the paradox of contemporary architecture

edited by peter cook, neil spiller, laura allen and peg rawes

WILEY-ACADEMY

First published in Great Britain in 2001 by
WILEY-ACADEMY

a division of
JOHN WILEY & SONS LTD
Baffins Lane
Chichester
West Sussex PO19 1UD

ISBN 0-471-49685-5

Other Wiley Editorial Offices
New York • Weinheim • Brisbane • Singapore • Toronto

Cover design: Christian Küsters, CHK Design, London
Series design: Christian Küsters, CHK Design, London
Cover and introduction photography: Paul Wesley Griggs

Layout and Prepress: ARTMEDIA PRESS Ltd, London

Printed and bound in Italy

porary

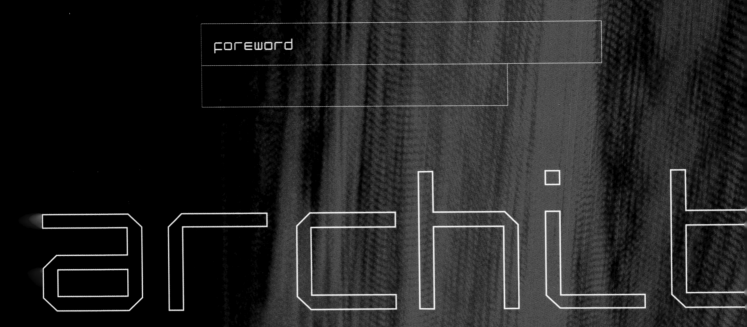

archit

Although I am the sponsor of the Lowe Lecture Series I am very flattered that Peter Cook should ask me to write the foreword to this second book. However, I am also aware that I must be careful in matters relating to the Lowe Lectures as they have been given by some of the world's most eminent architects. Moreover, this book will be read by students and practitioners who know far more about the subject than I do. So I would like to take this opportunity to explain why someone who is best known in the field of advertising should have chosen to sponsor a lecture series on architecture.

When I first went into advertising it was shortly after the beginnings of commercial television which, at the time, slavishly followed the American model with less than brilliant results.

For my own part, I quickly realised the importance of television advertising. For the first time, friends and children of friends (in fact virtually everybody), expressed an opinion about it; as TV advertising entered their homes it could not be ignored in the way that print advertising can. TV advertisements interfered with their favourite programmes, but more importantly many people found them grossly insulting, talking down to the audience as if it was somehow quite stupid.

Therefore I decided (along with a group of others of the late sixties generation) that we had to make advertising better; more lively, more interesting, more fun ... indeed often funny. And with the help of some fine copy-writers, art directors and a generation of TV directors, we gradually produced a new style of advertising which people actually liked and welcomed into their homes as a good part of the environment in which they lived.

It was about the same time that I met Brian Clarke and during one evening at dinner I apparently said to him that it was alright for him because if he created a bad piece of architectural design it was only in one place whereas my TV ads were seen by everyone. Of course in my naivety I forgot to consider – as Brian quickly pointed out – that my ads had a shelf life of about three months, whereas buildings have a shelf life of tens or hundreds of years. This is where my interest in architecture began; for if advertising could be a visual pollutant how much more so could poor design and architecture be?

I remember giving a lecture, around the same time, which started with photographs of the centres of London and Paris taken at the turn of the century, and compared these with the same view 75 years later. At the turn of the century we could see all the churches in both cities. In the later photograph of London only St. Paul's Cathedral remained, whereas Paris appeared to be virtually the same. Incidentally, for fear anyone should construe this as an attack on modern architecture, let me quickly dispel that thought. I am not against modern architecture, I am against horrid architecture.

My interest in architecture developed from these ideas and through my subsequent friendship with Norman Foster. I began slowly, but increasingly to realise that architects have a profession which, in the best cases, is close to a calling, for they design buildings which are not just functional but which have a real importance – uplifting or downgrading the environment – and thus in my view the spirit of the human race.

Throughout the course of my career I have travelled to most of the major cities of the world and in the course of those travels I have always tried to find time to spend a few hours or a day looking at the architecture of the cities. And I have found it extraordinary how architecture seems to have an effect on people's lives in so many ways.

The Italians eat well, dress well and have a permanent love of the creative arts. Could this be partly because of their history in architecture and design as well as music and painting? The Americans on the other hand, outside of the major cities or in many examples within them, tend to care less about these matters. Could this be

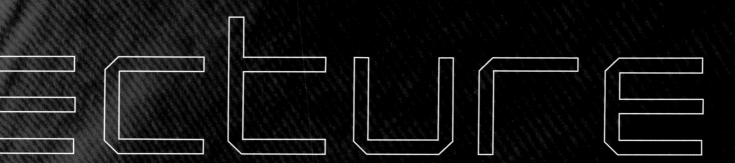

because so many of their main streets are so unspeakably ugly (no planning or zoning laws) crammed as they are with fast-food joints, gas stations, car showrooms and supermarkets, often sitting cheek-by-jowl with Baptist churches and brothels (suitably disguised of course)? Or could it be that all my colleagues in Barcelona are so cheerful and courteous because their spirit is just a little uplifted every day by the buildings of Gaudí? And could the aggression and lack of civility so prevalent in New York be because the size of the buildings make people feel like worker ants?

I should emphasise that I am not having 'a go' at American architecture which, in many cases, is some of the most brilliant in the world, but trying to illustrate that architecture and its role in the environment can and does have an enormous effect on people's behaviour and attitudes, just as sunshine or the lack of it also has an effect. It was for these reasons that I decided to sponsor the lectures which I hope people have enjoyed and been stimulated by.

Finally, can I thank all the people who have spoken and all the people who have listened for their interest and contribution.

Frank Lowe

introduction

Peter Cook and Neil Spiller

Following THE POWER OF CONTEMPORARY ARCHITECTURE, this is the second volume based on the Lowe Lectures at the Bartlett School of Architecture, London, inspired and supported by the internationally creative Lowe Group. Fundamental to Frank Lowe's contribution to British culture is his discovery and support of talent, a fascination that is reflected at the Bartlett. We are similarly intrigued by the interactive effect of one mind upon another. We are constantly seeking out people who can continue to tweak the rest of us, making us aware of creative alternatives, and hopefully, leaving us not only a little bit less comfortable, but itching to do something ourselves.

Neil Spiller: The Lowe Group's generous support of this international lecture series has created another focus in architectural discourse. How does it differ from what is on offer elsewhere in the UK and across Europe?

Peter Cook: It's less consciously based on reputation than most lecture series, and it takes more risks than, say, the RIBA's programme. It's less politically correct than the Architectural Association's series; more international than Columbia's. I still watch the Oslo weekly series list, out of the corner of my eye; the guys up there have fronted 30 years of lectures of an extraordinary range – and the high standard of built work in that city must have something to do with it. The major criterion for a lecture is IDEAS.

NS: Do you think that there is a new relationship between architectural theory and practice these days?

PC: My friends keep telling me there is, but my gut instinct runs to the opposite conclusion. I think people want there to be. So what we have is a lot of theoretical writing and commentary and the positing of abstract notions on the one hand, and then some other characters beavering away on some buildings, for good and even intellectually complex reasons – but this is considered architecture – not theory.

NS: Do you think this is an exciting time to be a practising architect or student? How does it differ from the atmosphere around the

Architectural Association in the late 1950s and early '60s, which, for my generation, seem like halcyon days?

PC: It's probably less different than you might think; a conscious 'avant-garde' in London existed then, despite the studied lack of interest from the Establishment and a curious mixture of puzzlement and embarrassment on the part of the students or contemporaries of those avant-garde people. Now, 'avant-garde' is a passé concept, but in a place like the Bartlett, there are several teacher-architects whose own work is out on a limb, and I make no secret of the fact that at least a third of our Lowe invitees are chosen as 'booster rockets' from the foreign pockets of the (unspoken) avant garde. On the other hand, when I read the weekly British architectural magazines, I sometimes despair: our local culture is very bleak in its neatness and politeness. Where are the young Smithsons? The embryonic Zaha Hadid? The next Cedric Price?

NS: Do you think many of our visiting architects would argue that context is 'bunk' in a global world, or would they argue for a revised notion of context?

PC: I think that Kenneth Frampton's 'Regionalism' was a cute excuse for delving into the byways of Modernism. 'Contextualism' is the prop of the third-rate local architect; so it is no surprise that many talented people search for an alternative. Our visitors are roughly divided between the universalist and the locally conscious, who see architecture itself as a parochial territory (and thus, context as well). Hans Hollein said in the

1960s, 'Alles ist Architektur', which is a healthy way out of the problem. I'm not sure about a 'revised notion of context' ... it's OK, so long as it doesn't become doctrinaire.

NS: Do you think that these architects represent a profession about to split, eg cybertects, corporate architects, web designers, etc?

PC: Maybe, yes, as part of a 'formal' profession, yet at the same time, as an area of study, architecture is attracting more and more of the intelligent young. Maybe it will end up as a creative baseline for myriad manifestations. TV and website design are only a beginning. This book presents alternatives: Stelarc is a performer; LOT/EK are creative responders; Marcos Novak is an alchemist; Oosterhuis is a weaver.

NS: Do you see this book as a section through architectural culture at a particular point in time, or is it more polemic?

PC: It is implicitly polemic: it suggests that exploration is central to architectural culture. It collects more iconoclasts than fellow travellers. It suggests that you should always be looking outwards. It's a thinly veiled criticism of 'politeness' in architecture.

NS: The Lowe lecturers form a close relationship with the school for a day or two. This is obviously crucial to us because it propagates the Bartlett ethos through first-hand experience.

PC: All means of propagation are crucial. This book gets into even more corners, taking with it the flavour of an ongoing discussion. It can also be used as a nudge-list for others to bring over speakers who will make an impact on their local scene. In the next few months, we shall bring twos and threes of our visitors together, not in an arch German-style 'podiumdiskussion', but in a naughty, infiltrationist way.

Peter Cook and Neil Spiller,
Bartlett School of Architecture,
London, September 2000

Mapping

Tarek Naga, the Cairo Project, a Vision
for an Emerging Cosmopolis, 2000

These days, many architects are incorporating geographical maps into their projects. These are not used in the sense of any projective geometry, but rather as tools of territorial modelling. The 'fold by fold' map makes it possible to superimpose and dovetail a whole host of conceptual references and data (semantic, sociological or climatic issues for example). New digital technologies are developing a world permeated by ebbs and flows, and by similarities in difference. Architecture is no longer taken as an object imposed on a territory; rather, it emanates from its many varied transformations.

The new concepts of 'morphogenesis of place' have opened the geographical map up to a new transformational dimension. In 1930, Richard Buckminster Fuller's 'Dymaxion' map was presented as a chart of movements in a new, globalised horizon. In the late 1950s, the geographical map enabled Constant to draw up an ever-different territory of 'New Babylon', developing with the trajectory of its inhabitants. It also enabled Yona Friedman to devise an 'artificial topography' with 'Spatial Cities', suspended on stilts, in which the manmade landscape is an inhabitable map. Today, MVRDV's 'Datatowns' are radicalising Friedman's proposition by turning the city into layers of data and information systems, with the loss of any original referent.

A far-reaching exploration of the concept of surface has transformed both architecture and the geographical map. Ideas of layer, envelope, surface coiling and uncoiling, and rising ground are put forward as active, process-based fields. These 'surfacings' are a flexible and abstract form of mapping, between the tracing and the cast, retaining the planar dimension of a smooth sheet, where the world's movements continuously fan out. No one describes this approach better than Neil Denari: 'The world, in terms of technology, is more like a map than a real sphere. Perhaps it could even be called a graph where information is more important than how many square miles of land a country or a city has'. In Denari's 1996 installation at the Gallery MA in Tokyo, the inner surfaces are folded and deformed, turned down like 'interrupted' projection-mapping planes, stripped of all geographical information. They form a complex geometric space, smooth like a sheet or map, without any referent. The exploration of these new, digital, map-like territories has enabled architecture to become 'another global surface'.

François Roche sees architecture as affected by many different factors – social, economic, sensory, territorial. For him, drawing up an operative mapping of a territory is tantamount to potentially erecting an architecture, seen as 'management of differentiated flows'. In 'Fractal City' (project for Rotterdam, 1998), it is the raised areas of ground that become architecture; here, the architecture is at once a singular territory and an artificialised nature. Architecture – an unstable consistency, and a forever renewed metabolism – has to do with a dialectic between map and territory, which might almost be compared to Robert Smithson's definition of 'sites' and 'non-sites', somewhere between territorial inscription and plan.

Actar Arquitectura and Vicente Guallart also define their projects as 'operative maps'. Recourse to mapping and fractal geometries enables them to link local and global, and to turn the representation of territory into an evolving grid on differing scales. We can thus say that, for them, the map is a 'metaterritory', and territory a 'metamap'. Fractal geometries developed similarities between the local and the global, between ontologically separate entities, but ones that are brought together by the structural osmosis of the fractal and its ever-changing methods of representation.

A sort of simultaneity in time and space is ushered in as a result of the vector-based, logical systems of mapping, which sidestep the object as much as the mimetic order of representation. What the map henceforth measures is no longer something real that takes precedence over its modelling. In the projects of Greg Lynn,

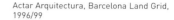

Actar Arquitectura, Barcelona Land Grid, 1996/99

Asymptote, Roche, Actar and Guallart, not forgetting Tarek Naga, the map is a 'metastratum', which is formed simultaneously by the real and its modelling. The one evolves with the other, without any discontinuity. The map has become a topological surface that stems as much from the 'landscape' as from its 'topography', as Lynn proposes. This space-time dynamic is perhaps per se an aesthetic and conceptual revolution, as Cubism was for the artistic avant-gardes, injecting forms with simultaneity, and as Futurism was too, endowing them with movement and a new kind of cinematics. The geographical map is now a changing graph, which has turned into an 'active' architecture.

Translated by Simon Pleasance

meLviln charney

Tracking Images : The News as Muse

PARABLE NO. 11... so be it, 1992
Oil pastel and acrylic on photograph
and on paper, mounted on masonite
244 x 122 cm
Collection: National Gallery of Canada
(Photo: courtesy Sable-Castelli Gallery,
Toronto)

In 1970, in response to a competition for the design of an Air Force memorial and museum, it seemed to me relevant to base the design on available sources derived from a world radically altered by technology. A flight map found in the seat pocket of an aircraft therefore becomes a network of museum facilities in several cities; sites consecrated by the loss of lives in air crashes locate memorials.

Often, this evidence originated in international media images showing buildings and cities caught up in news events, which I began to collect and classify. Events attribute a cachet of consequences to hapless structures caught in an instant of celebrity or, more likely, disaster. They also undermine what appears self-evident, and expose a subterfuge of supports and links. The images reveal these underlying associations, evoking a system of classification that assumes the character of a 'dictionary', in so far as a recurring series of images constitutes a record of common meaning: a record of discernible interaction between people and constructs, and within a system of constructs itself.

An initial series introduces the capacity of events to propel buildings and cities into our consciousness. Their impact on physical structures is noted; buildings and cities are in a state of flux, as if events take place to lay bare the human effort interred in built formations. 'Series 10–19' gathers images concerning the internal order of built formations. Undifferentiated frames and grids, along with figural tropes, appear to have an autonomous life of their own, as if it is their vocation to do so. 'Series 20–29' concentrates on models of buildings and cities in the hands of people in power; the size of the models varying inversely with the degree of power they exercise – the more tenuous it is, the greater the dimensions of the models that overwhelm their progenitors. 'Series 30–39' highlights complementary mechanisms of control, the enforcement of a fragmented view of the world by men in uniform who rivet our attention to mere particles – a door or a gutter – rather than to their actions. 'Series 40–49' details a world of exclusion and effacement, where people are also in direct physical contact with the built world, but they are trapped in its minutiae and reduced to vague blurs suspended in a hiatus of time and place. The final series gathers images of people reclaiming their time and place. The excluded are seen floundering in the effluence of advanced industrial societies in a cruel replay of deeply

rooted and elemental human impulses – Adam's eternal struggle to rebuild his house in paradise; over-populated cities cruising the face of the earth like so many Noah's Arks.

'Un Dictionnaire' shifts one's focus from the singularity of an event to its place in the changing world. Disasters and celebrations fuse in a single, all-embracing reality. One is not certain whether buildings and cities are going up or coming down. What is certain is a sense of pervasive turmoil, and that in the midst of this turmoil people manifest their existence in built form. Such gestures are still capable of reaching us.

'Un Dictionnaire' maintains the thematic focus of my work:

• From the initial concept for an Air Force memorial and museum, to a series of worked-over photographs documenting air flight, to constructions dropping out from images of aircraft in the news, the 'In Flight Series, 1990-94', reposition a radical strain.

• From a series of constructions picking up on edgy tabloid images, to urban insertions creating events in the news – such as at Les Maisons de la rue Sherbrooke (1976) – to a garden for the Canadian Center for Architecture (1987–91) – a construction of superposed portraits of gardens and buildings drawn out of the site and its immediate (tabloid) surroundings, these works cut an edge between disciplinary boundaries, between constructed objects as fact and fiction.

The various threads of this work are picked up in the recent 'Parable Series'. If 'Un Dictionnaire' digs at an opaque wall of surfeit meaning promulgated by news photos in an attempt to march viewers through reflexes numbed by the constant exposure to each day's crop of media

In Flight... Sélavy, No. 2, 1990
Wood, partially painted
292 x 442 x 880 cm
Installation View: The Canadian Center for
Architecture, Montréal, 1991-2
Collection: Fonds National d'Art
Contemporain, Paris
(Photo: courtesy Canadian Center for
Architecture)

Canadian Center for Architecture Garden:
view of the Esplanade from the Arcade
wirh six of the ten Allegoric Columns
(Photo: Robert Burley; collection:
Canadian Center for Architecture)

images, 'Parables' unravel the totemic space of the images themselves. These are taken to be 'sites' bearing the imprint of human constructs and desires: sites where we may excavate a sense of 'presentness', to grasp being 'here' now.

Aarhus Horizon - A Dynamic Masterplan for the
Redevelopment of the Harbour Area, Aarhus,
Denmark, 2000

Aarhus Horizon, detail

Next page:
Aarhus Horizon, plan

Conflict

The proposed extension of the harbour creates an increase in economic and other potential, but is also generating major conflicts.

Urban Prototypes

Conflicts generate new possibilities if they are given a vehicle by which to transform their energies. Such a vehicle is an urban prototype. Urban prototypes are instruments for dynamic change; they reorganise existing local conditions and link them to the potential offered by global developments.

Horizon

Coincidental with the harbour extension, space between the harbour and the city is becoming free or needs restructuring. This space offers unique opportunities: to create a new horizon for Aarhus, a line, a threshold, a clear mark dividing city and harbour, city and sea. The simplicity of this line is a new symbol for Aarhus, an invitation to reorganise its exchange with the sea, to create a perspectival vision of future dynamics.

Threshold and Cut

As threshold, the horizon links marine life, sea trade, oceans, vastness, with close-knit communities, domesticity, the dense mass of buildings of a city, land and agriculture. As a cut it separates more clearly city from harbour.

Public Space as Instrument

The Horizon is a public space, an instrument for dynamic change. This instrument redefines, re-regulates, capitalises on existing conditions, and invites new programmes to intermingle with them. It generates the connectivity between programmes needed for a truly dynamic environment. The Horizon belongs to all, yet is used differently by each. Its added value is to link those different uses together to create new urban life.

Line, Landmark

The line stretches from Risskov to Marselisborg, touching the inner harbour and marking the river mouth. It is the main landmark of Aarhus. To etch this line into the urban fabric and public consciousness, the Aarhus Festival will expand its range and scale of activities. Existing and new events will take place on and around the line. For example, every second year, a selection of well-known architects will build a temporary structure somewhere along the line.

The Urban Gallery

The Horizon as an instrument is played by inserting elements from the Urban Gallery. This consists of a collection of programmes, actions, events and objects that are grouped in a taxonomy of four layers: Branding, Earth, Flow and Incorporation.

Engines of Change

Although programmes of each layer can occupy the line independently, combined, they create new possibilities, engines of change. The Horizon is a single path, a park, a traffic machine, a viewing terrace, a transferium, a new city edge. These engines rely upon industrial expansion and development, the success of the Aarhus Festival, other developments such as new forms of urban transport, ecological awareness, the place of sport and outdoor leisure in city culture, reforms in education and new technologies, such as information processing and sewage treatment.

Dynamic Masterplan, an Urban Toolbox

Aarhus and its harbour require a dynamic masterplan formed by the Horizon as instrument and the Urban Gallery as a programmatic toolbox. The Aarhus Horizon is the concrete side of the gallery, and sets up the common space that links

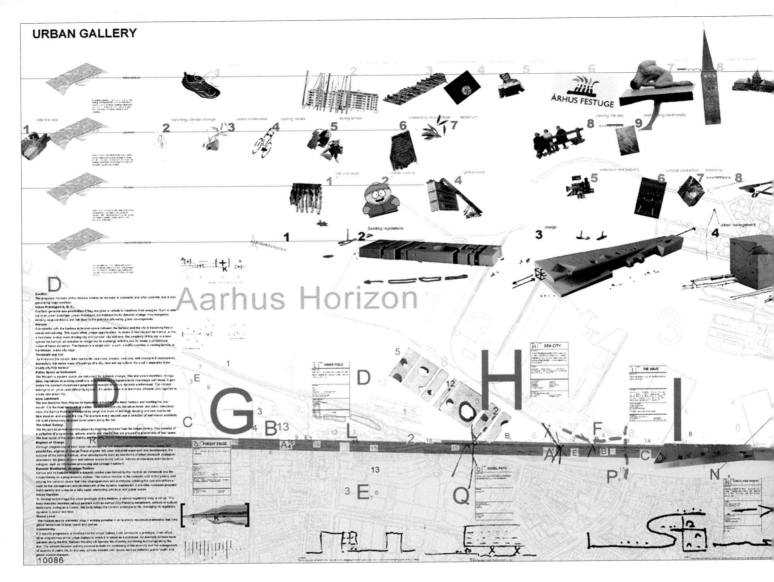

Aarhus Horizon

10086

all programmes and prototypes, creating the operational framework for the management and development of the dynamic masterplan. It provides increased programmatic density and pulse on a daily basis, interacting with local and global scales.

Urban Curation
To develop and manage the urban prototype of the Horizon, a special regulatory body is set up. This mediates between various partners such as Aarhus City Planning Department, schools, or cultural institutions. Acting as a curator, this body brings the Horizon prototype to life, managing its regulatory dynamic in space and time.

Global Local
The Horizon and its elements plug in to existing potential in an explicitly reciprocal relationship that links global tendencies to local needs and desires.

Connectivity
If a specific programme is inserted into the Urban Gallery, it will connect to a prototype, and will affect other programmes of the Urban Gallery to which it is linked. For example, schools have gardens along the line. Harbour industry will sponsor biodiversity-monitoring technology along the line. The schools become involved in both the monitoring of biodiversity and the management of aspects of public life. In this way, schools interlink with issues such as pollution, public health and global climate changes.

Branding
Branding contains conditions of naming, marketing, creating identity, cultural production, memory, remembrance, creating values and the communication of these values, images and imaginary conditions, narration and scripting.

Earth
Earth contains conditions of the land, waters, the air, natural processes, ecological issues, biodiversity, but also land and landownership, territory, and rights concerning the surface of the earth, spatial organisation.

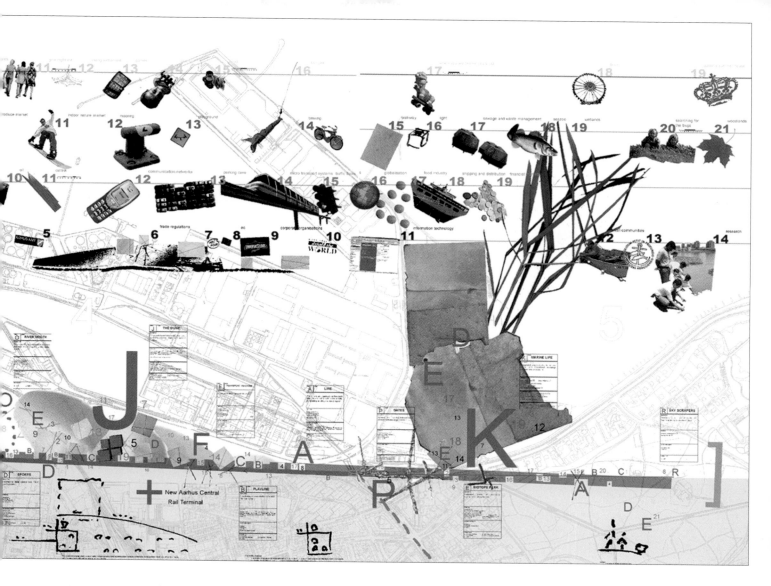

Flow
Money, traffic, displacement of people, goods, information, mobility, waste, sewage, the economy of the site. Flow contains all processes that create flows through the Urban Gallery.

Incorporation
Incorporation includes political actions and constellations, institutions and institutionalisation, community formation, organisations of various kinds, groups, legal bodies, legal actions.

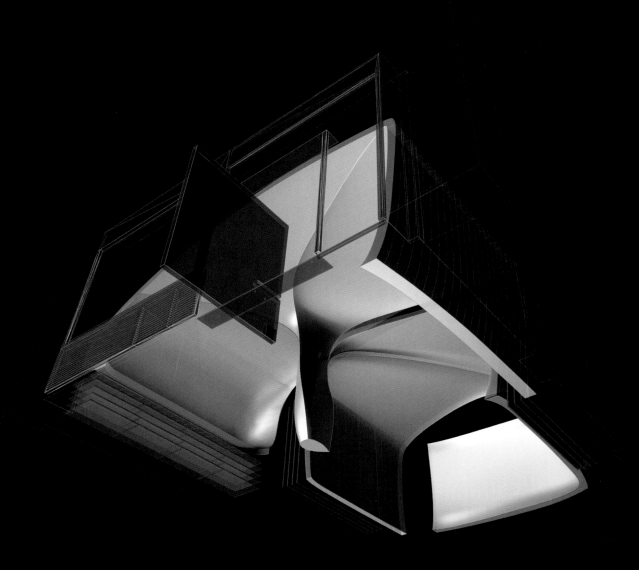

Three Projects: Aegis (1999-2001), Paramorph (1999), The Blue Gallery (1999-2000)

The Blue Gallery (1999-2000)

The most profound societal change of the past 50 years has been the transition from the norms of an industrialised society to those of a society of mass communication. The most fundamental architecture of the present is therefore the zillions of channels of communication that have been opened, which offer multiple possibilities for local dialect and spontaneity. Social structure is less organised on models of efficiency, or even of nationality, than it is by the endless creation of identity, through products, advertising, etc. This marks our time as an essentially ornamental one, in which there is a re-emergence of notions of aesthetics, but seen, not so much formally as socially, as a discourse of shared appreciation. In a time of branding and product identity, there is a need for a sort of social semiotics to account for the effectiveness of such electronic strategy – of the generation and maintenance of concepts of identity. Aesthetics, for Habermas or Marcuse, for instance, is that discourse that asks how it is that a given community can mutually identify with some object or act in order to reinforce its own sense of identity.

This is no simple return to a pre-industrial sensibility, for such an aesthetics is heterotopic rather than utopic, sanctioned by a 'design' fervour that has become divorced from the determinism and idealism of early 20th-century thought. 'Design', held to be the enhancement of living conditions through rational re-evaluation of quotidian life (evident across the political spectrum from Marxism to Fascism), dissolves into myriad ornamental practices.

Given the essentially ephemeral nature of such transition in cultural pattern, it is difficult to discern the specificity of its effect on architecture. Rather, such change demands a re-thinking of a still highly egotistical and individual mode of practice, and of the singularity of architectural aesthetics, rooted as it is in utopian discourse and frequently in a formalist rather than social perspective. We look to devising entirely different modes of practice that conjure works responsive to a new technological state.

We have included three projects under the 'Paradox of Contemporary Architecture' theme. The Aegis and Paramorph projects have not been 'designed' as such, but have emerged from the establishment of a series of parameters that announce not so much a project, as the very possibility of a project. Both offer themselves as examples of

'An Architecture of Reciprocity', the Aegis hypersurface literally deforming in response to the proximity of people, and the fluid form of the Paramorph as a gateway-in-depth, envisaged as an interactive aural chamber responsive to the flow of people passing through. Both projects offer hints of an architecture of indeterminacy, in which the aesthetic derives not as an auto-didactic 'design' flourish but as a mode of environmental malleability; time becoming infiltrated in a now social aesthetic. This is to look for fresh ways of deploying the evident power of electronics into new forms of tactile experience, and it will be interesting to gauge the response that such active forms carry.

The Blue Gallery addresses more directly the question of 'affect', since it was condemned, despite its delicacy, for its aesthetic presence, overbearing to the contemporary artists who were due to use it. Here, too, we have attempted to devise a form of reciprocity: the gallery that would lightly demand an interaction from the artists and artworks that were to inhabit it in subjecting the apparent 'neutrality' of the ubiquitous white box to interrogation. But just three days after its inauguration it was destroyed, as if the challenge it offered was unsanctionable by the artists.

As the product of a genuinely communal act of creativity, and a quite subtle expression of a new formal aesthetic made possible by CAD technology, such an act raises many questions as to the power of contemporary architecture, and its ability to reveal the outline of the often invisible cultural limits that surround us. Architecture remains, for us, one of the most powerful forms of expression possible, a visceral form of memory now become profligate, responsive.

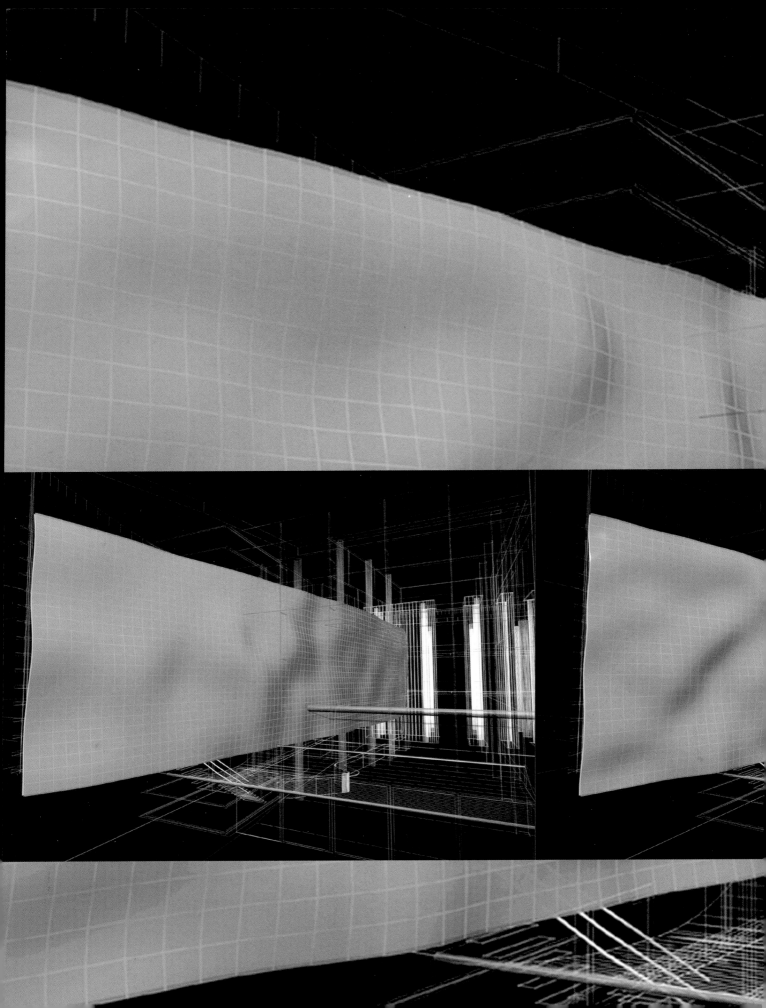

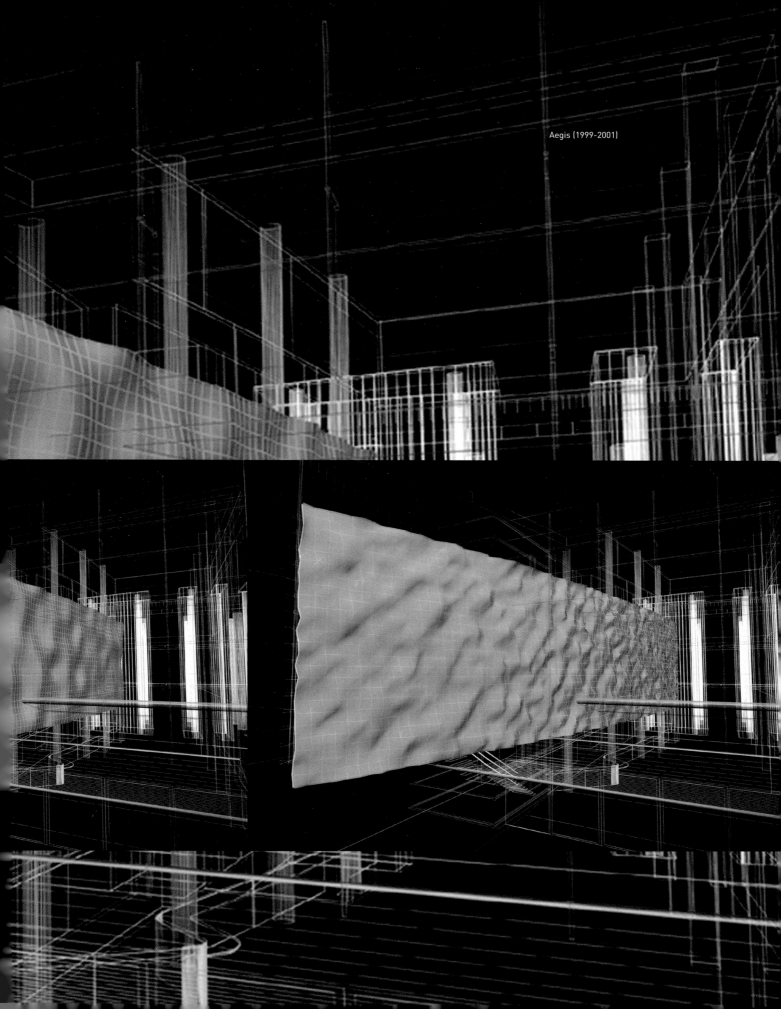

Aegis (1999-2001)

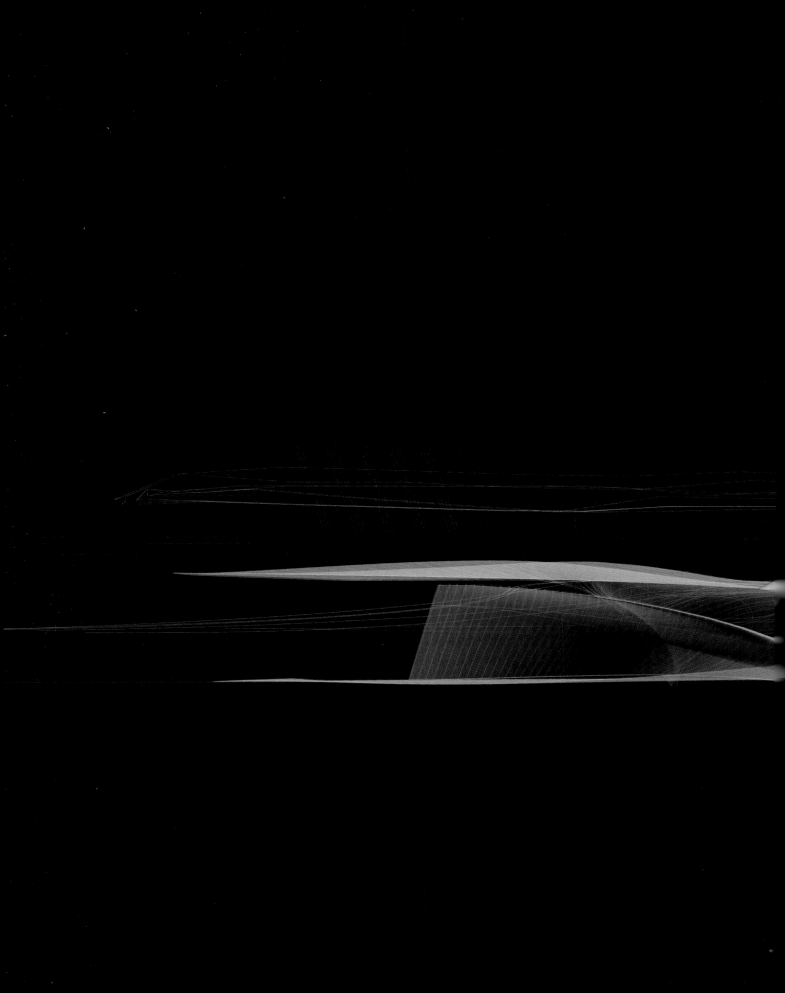

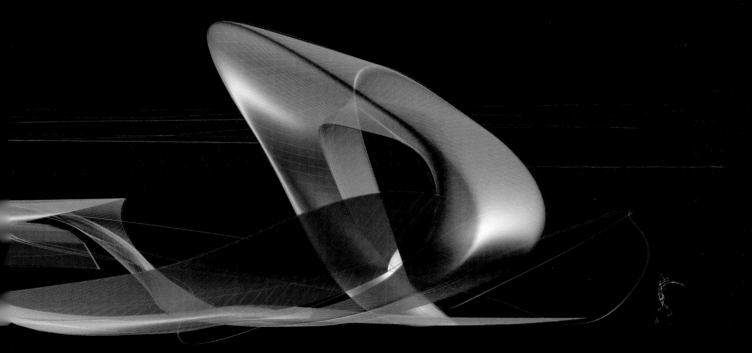

Paramorph (1999)

Architectural Concept and Urban Strategy:
Staging the Field of Possibilities

Centre for Contemporary
Arts, Rome (1999): painting

The Centre for Contemporary Arts, Rome, addresses the question of its urban context by maintaining an indexicality to the former army barracks. This is in no way an attempt at topological pastiche, but instead continues the low-level urban texture set against the higher level blocks on the surrounding sides of the site. At times, it affiliates with the ground to become new ground, yet also ascends and coalesces to become massivity where needed. The entire building has an urban character. Prefiguring a directional route connecting the river to Via Guido Reni, the Centre encompasses the movement patterns both extant and desired, contained within and outside. This vector defines the primary entry route into the building. By intertwining the circulation with the urban context, the building shares a public dimension with the city, overlapping tendril-like paths and open space. In addition to the circulatory relationship, the architectural elements are also geometrically aligned with the urban grids that join at the site. In partly deriving its orientation and physiognomy from the context, it further assimilates itself to the specific conditions of the site.

Space versus Object
Our purpose offers a quasi-urban field, a 'world' to dive into rather than a building as signature object. The campus is organised and navigated on the basis of directional drifts and the distribution of densities rather than key points. This is indicative of the character of the Centre as a whole: porous, immersive, a field space.

An inferred mass is subverted by vectors of circulation. The external as well as the internal circulation follows the overall drift of the geometry. Vertical and oblique circulation elements are located at areas of confluence, interference and turbulence. The move from object to field is critical in understanding the relationship that the architecture will have to the content of the artwork it will house. Whilst this is further expounded by the contributions of our gallery and exhibitions experts, it is important here to state that the premise of the architectural design promotes a disinheriting of the object-orientated gallery space. Instead, the notion of a 'drift' takes on an embodied form. The drifting emerges, therefore, as both architectural motif and a way in which to navigate experimentally through the museum. It is an argument that in art practice is well understood, but in architectural hegemony has

remained alien. We take this opportunity, in the adventure of designing such a forward-looking institution, to confront the material and conceptual dissonance evoked by art practice since the late 1960s. The path leads away from the 'object' and its correlative sanctification, towards fields of multiple associations that anticipate the necessity to change.

Institutional Catalyst
As such, it is deemed significant that in configuring the possible identity of this newly established institution (housing both art and architecture), with its aspiration towards the polyvalent density of the 21st century, conceptions of space and indeed temporality are reworked. Modernist utopian space fuelled the white 'neutrality' of most 20th-century museums. Now, this disposition must be challenged, not simply out of wilful negation, but by the necessity for architecture to continue its critical relationship with contemporary social and aesthetic categories. Since absolutism has been indefinitely suspended from current thought on the issue of art presentation, it is towards the idea of the 'maximising exhibition' that we gravitate. In this scenario, the Centre makes primary the manifold possibilities for the divergence in showing art and architecture as well as catalysing the discourse on its future. Again, the 'signature' aspect of an institution of this calibre is sublimated into a more pliable and porous organism that promotes several forms of identification at once.

Wall/Not-Walls: Towards a Contemporary Spatiality
In architectural terms, this is most virulently

gallery, the visitor experiences the interplay between the strictly orthogonal design of these structures, and the organic body of the hall. This space serves as a transition from daylight and foyer light to artificial light. The high, open and brightly lit space between the outer facades and the main foyer is fractured by bridges, from which one can view and appreciate the building's interior.

In the basement of the Festival Hall, on the same level as the underground car park, are technical rooms and a delivery zone for the stage and storerooms. The foyer, which is on the same level as Schubert Square, can be reached directly via the car park by stairs and an escalator.

The aim of the interior design was to realise the ideal concert hall, which could offer the perfect setting for opera, musicals, concerts or ballet, with only a few technical alterations. These variations are achieved through foldable ceiling mechanisms and rotating wall elements for lighting, horizontal and vertical alteration of the stage opening, and extension of the stage surface far into the auditorium.

A 'shell' serves as a diaphragm between stage and auditorium, defining the space for the performers and providing an essential acoustic element. In order to guarantee the uniformity of the concert space beyond the metal curtain into the auditorium, its shape is a continuation of the walls and the structured ceiling of the hall.

A hall should not only offer optimal acoustic conditions, but should also provide a physically pleasant space. Here, the near-rectangular design consists of a rising parquet area and a gallery of the same material, which, due to its green wall with strong cobalt blue elements, stands out clearly against the parquet; a central gallery,

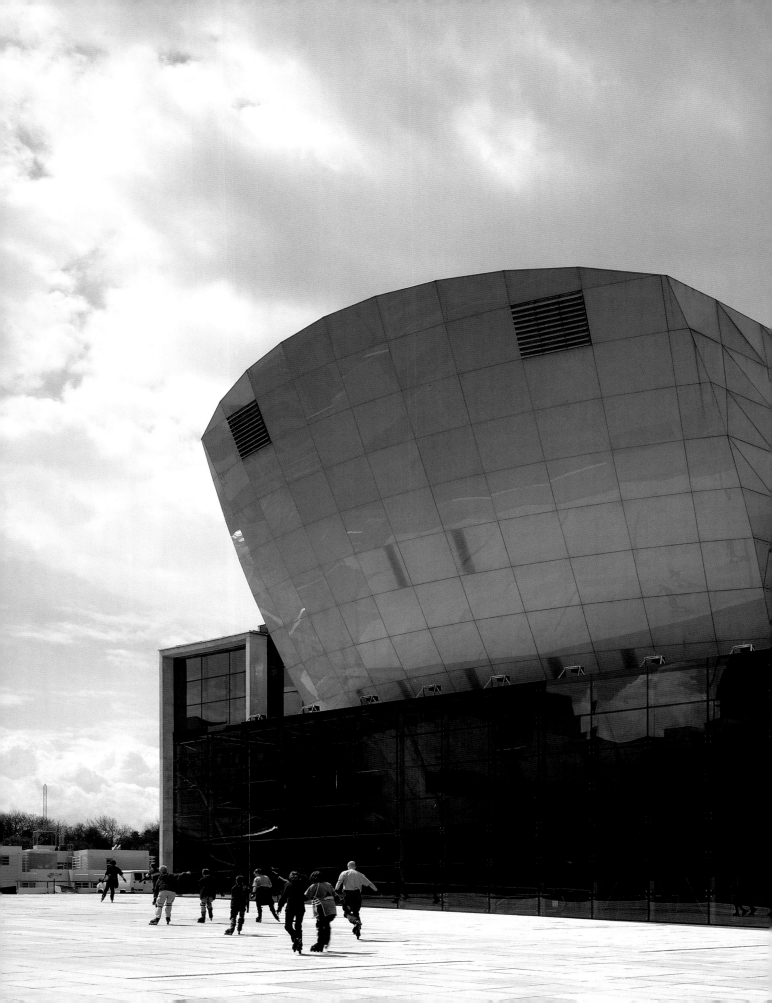

accessible from the upper floor; and the two side galleries. These are extended up to the orchestra pit, shifting the musical activity towards the centre of the auditorium, subdividing the high wall surfaces and improving the acoustics. Seats with black and light-grey striped covers stand on a blackish parquet flooring made of wenge (a tropical wood).

Separated from the auditorium, artists' rooms and administration area, the stage can be reached directly from the square level and from the underground car park. With a flexible 10 x 20 metre opening, it consists of main, side, back and apron and incorporates a stage house. In front of this is an orchestra pit with flexible platform divided into two parts and a transportation platform within the stage. Travelling light towers for the portal and a two-storey portal lighting bridge that can be raised and lowered are designed to adjust the proscenium, whilst an iron curtain weighing almost 15 tons separates stage and auditorium.

Colours are determined by the materials used and mainly consist of pale shades in various glass and metal surfaces. These reflect and absorb light, creating various nuances, accentuations and atmospheres in different daylight and artificial light conditions.

A second space is provided by the 250-seat Haydnsaal, designed in a flexible manner so that it can serve as a hall for chamber concerts, exhibitions, readings, theatre and other events. Its cobalt blue, scale-like glass cladding and cubic form make it stand out like another gem from the agglomeration of peripheral buildings, dominating on its slim pillars. Its functionality is considerably enriched by the potential to adjust the acoustics by means of folding panels, which extend fully to the ceiling, and to vary the natural lighting through skylights and windows.

On the west side facing the city and partially on the south side, the stage tower is completed by a rampant seven-storey section. Three storeys house the artists' dressing rooms, rehearsal rooms etc, whilst above them are administration and technical management (Schönbergsaal) and a ballet room (Sternensaal). Both are suitable for multipurpose use. The outer wall of the stage tower, which is made of the same material throughout, acts as a guiding wall, facilitating clear orientation.

Credits

Project team: Ursula Märzendorfer, Erwin Matzer, Peter Rous, Willi Nakolnig, Heribert Altenbacher, Peter Szammer, Alexander Forathofer, Wolfgang Wimmer, Frank Moritz, Robert Clerici, Ronald Schatz, Herbert Schwarzmann, Elisabeth Kopeinig, Claudia Schmidt, Michael Gattermeyer, Ellen Klanek, Roswitha Küng-Freiberger, Hubert Schuller.

Structural consultant: Helmut Zieritz

Knots and Networks

Knots are static or dynamic data resources that serve as spaces for the processing or storing of data. Performers process the data collected in the knots and communicate with other performers. Performers can be either people or machines, both processing information located in the different knots of the network.[1]

In many ways, networks function as mediators between the physical world and the non-material scenarios of the projected, virtual realm of information. Like fishermen, we gather the goods and information that we need to survive in both the physical and the virtual realms of our lives. Whether we collect seafood, catch butterflies or collect information via the Internet, we employ our nets and filters to make the invisible visible, to distinguish the necessary from the superfluous as much as to establish interactive connections.

The key terms of the Internet economy, which transforms information into money and by turn purchases physical and virtual products, are 'performers' and 'knots'. The latter term has its origin in the traditional craft of net making. Today, it is associated with the coming together of information highways, leading to a layering of information at the control centres of worldwide operating networks.

The universally standardised format of computer screens might be a cause for the similarity in the content of information being processed and transmitted. The lack of diversity in the format of the transmitted information on the web might also be one of the reasons for society's orientation problems. Therefore it may be necessary to counteract the virtual knots of information with the creation of meaning in the physical world.

At a time when our perception is exposed to an ever-increasing number of projections, it might be that 'knots of meaning' in the physical world could create awareness and orientation. These knots are significant places of experience for our perception, as for instance Walter de Maria's LIGHTNING FIELD (1977), the Calendar buildings in Jaipur, India, or the Neanderthal Museum (1994-6), which is situated in a recreational area between Düsseldorf, Mettmann and Wuppertal in Germany. The museum's task is to present Neanderthal artefacts, many of which have been destroyed over the years due to quarrying in the area.

The Jahrtausendblick (Millennium View) in Steinbergen can be seen in the same context. The staircase building, which overlooks a quarry, is a reminder of the staircase in Babel destroyed by Xerxes in order to weaken the belief of the people of Babylon.

As a 'knot of meaning' the Jahrtausendblick does not stand for the reincarnation of Classical beliefs or worldviews. It stands as a sign for the beginning of a new era. A space consisting of ten glass frames seemingly floats on top of the staircase, marking the beginning of the information age.

Translated by Torsten Schmiedeknecht

Reference
Ben Goertzel and John Pritchard, 'Die Internet-Ökonomie als komplexes System', FRANKFURTER ALLGEMEINE ZEITUNG, 17 March 2000, p 53.

Neanderthal Museum: exterior and interior

Lot/EH

Urban Scan

ABSENCE all-purpose amnesia
bald banal bare
basic blank careless
common desert empty
exposed faceless GENERIC
indefinite institutional lack
less marginal naked
nameless non-classified non-descript
nothingness nowhere NUDE
obvious off ordinary
raw reveal SCATTERED
secondary sparse sporadic
stripped transparent uninhabited
unrefined unsophisticated utilitarian
vacant vacuum vague
versatile VOID zero

absorb accumulate add-on
adhere adopt ALIEN
annex acquire amass
assimilate bury climb
cling contagious contaminate
embed embody ENCAPSULATE
enclose extraneous fill
immerge incorporate incubate
INFEST infiltrate inject
insert intercept interfere
intersect intrude invade
jut-out merge nidification
occupy OVERLAP parasite
penetrate perturb perforate
permeate pierce prosthesis
protrude protuberance saturate
STRATIFY sunk swallow
tentacular VIRUS wrap

acentric antigravity antithesis
ASLANT contradict contrary
counterclockwise crooked dare
decentralise defy deficient
deregulate despite DISCORDANCE
disestablish disproportionate disregard

dissymetric illegal illegitimate
illicit illogical IMPERTINENT
inappropriate incorrect indecent
imperfect imprecise impure
inadequate incoherent inaccurate
insufficient IRREGULAR irregularity
limp oblique subvert
tilted UNBALANCED unequal
uneven unstable vertigo

ACCELERATE bypass cinematic
circulate commute drive-in
drive-thru drop-off DYNAMIC
emigrate errant erratic
express fast fast-food
FAST-FORWARD flash hectic
homelessness immigrant jammed
jump kinetic manoeuvre
MOBILE mobility movement
motion navigate nomad
orbit oscillate path
rush rhythm shortcut
spin stir TAKE-OFF
traffic transit transport
trajectory vagrant vector
vehicle velocity WANDER

abrupt alternating brief
CHANGEABLE cyclic discontinuous
ephemeral expired evanescent
immediate IMPERMANENT incomplete
inconstant in-progress instant
instantaneously interim intermittent
interrupted momentary now
ONGOING phase present
prop-up recurrent sudden
temporary transient transitory
unfinished variable VANISHING

ACCESSORISED air-conditioned airtight
appliance apparatus automatic
built-in capsule COLLAPSIBLE

comfortable compact compartmentalised
convenient CONVERTIBLE customised
efficient electric electronic
enjoy ERGONOMIC futuristic
gadgeted hydraulic hygienic
hyperfunctional immunised INSULATED
mechanical microhabitat motorised
MOVABLE multifunctional multipurpose
niche padded plug-in
pneumatic portable pop-up
push-button reclinable reversible
SELF-CONTAINED self-operating self-starting
self-supporting useful useless
waterproof water-resistant WATER-TIGHT

assemble ASSEMBLAGE assembly-line
attach brand combine
COMPATIBLE component connect
disassemble element format
interchangeable install join
kit MODULAR part
prefab procedure process
prototype READY-MADE model
reassemble reattachable replaceable
STACKABLE standard standardisation
system type UNIT

ACCIDENTAL adventure appetite
arbitrary by-product casual
chain-reaction challenge CHANCE
CHAOS coincidence curious
desire discover doubt
eager emergency encounter
error EVENT experiential
experimental explore happen
hint imaginary improvise
incident ingenious instinct
INVOLUNTARY lapsus mistake
multiple-choice obsessive obstinate
occasion occur phenomenon
probability prone RANDOM
relativism snap uncertain

UNEXPECTED unexplored unintentional
unplanned unpredictable UNPREMEDITATED

alphabet ANNOUNCEMENT advertisement
barcode billboard binarycode
chart codify cross-reference
DATA database decipher
decode detect diagram
digital digitalise DIRECTIONS
download graph graphics
index information initialise
input INSTRUCTIONS itemise
interpret list map
media numbering pixel
plan programme scan
scheme scroll select
sign SIGNAGE subtitles
tabulated tag WARNING

abstract ABSTRACTION apparition
assumption brain cerebral
code CONCEPT conceptual
conceptualise concoct core
dream essence essential
FANTASY formula geometry
hallucination hypothetical idea
ideal IMAGINARY intellectual
intention invent INVENTION
logical mental metaphor
rational scheme symbolic
theory theoretical THOUGHT
transcendent type typical
unapplied unpractical VISION
visionary visual VISUALISE

alter AMPLIFY bisect
break change chop
clip compact COMPRESS
concentrate condense consolidate
CROP cut cut-off
cut-out detach DILATE
divide edit elongate

enhance enlarge expand
extend extrude flip
fold FREEZE half
increase lengthen magnify
maximise minimise move
offset reduce RETRACT
rotate scale section
separate SHRINK squeeze
split stitch STRETCH

AGGLOMERATE coexist confusion
congestion cohabit conurbation
cosmopolis crowd DENSITY
disorder disorient ENDLESS
enormous exchange interact
interconnect loud mass
mass-media MASS-PRODUCTION mass-transportation
megalopolis mess metropolis
multicentred MULTICOLOURED multicultural
multiethnic MULTIFORM multilayered
multilingual MULTIRACIAL multitude
noise overbuilt overgrown
overstimulate overwhelm SPRAWLING
suburban urban URBANISED

ACCESS airline airmail
antenna audio broadcast
cable cell-phone channel
communicate CONNECTION dial-tone
e-mail enter exit
frequency GLOBALISATION hub
interface keyboard keypad
link mesh monitor
MULTICHANNEL multidimensional multidirectional
multimedia net NETWORK
node online on-screen
radar SATELLITE signal
simulcast surveillance technology
telecommunication terminal touch-tone
TRANSMISSION video-conferencing wave-length
web wireless WORLDWIDE

ACTIVATE addict affect
agitate amaze amusing
ANIMATE appeal attract
captivate capture compel
drive ENGAGE engaging
entertain excite exploit
funny hooked impact
impel INDUCE influence
initiate instigate interrogative
intrigue launch MOTIVATE
pressure PROMPT provoke
push spur stimulate
surprise TRIGGER urge

ADAPT alienate appropriate
associate borrow commute
CONVERT derivation DERIVATIVE
disarrange disassociate disconnect
DISPLACE estrange excavate
extract export found
import JUXTAPOSE manipulate
metamorphosis migrate misappropriate
modify MUTATE mutant
permutate reconfigure remove
rename replace RETHINK
reuse reverse shift
stranger transfer transmutation
TRANSFORM transpose update

ARTIFICIAL clone computerised
copy counterfeit DUPLICATE
facsimile icon image
illusion imitate iterate
microchip MULTIPLE record
render repeat replicant
reproduce robotisation SAMPLING
serialisation similitude simulation
simulator simultaneous substitution
surrogate SYNTHETIC synonymous
synthesised VIRTUAL video
voice-activated xerox ZOOM

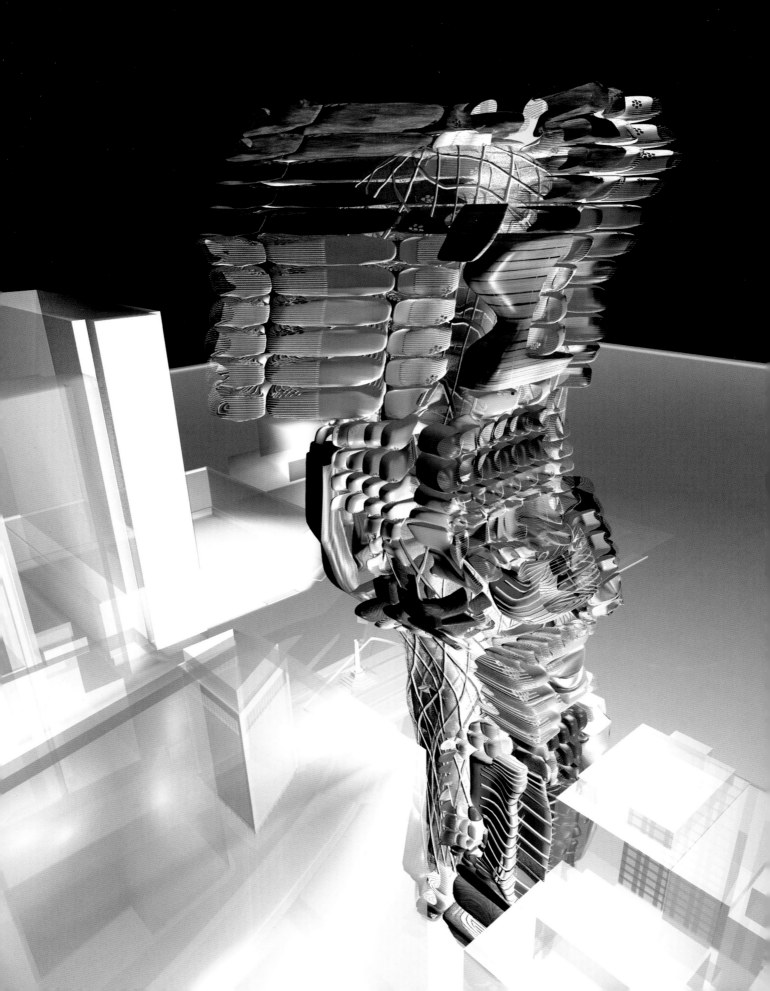

Jahrtausendblick (Millennium View),
1997-2000

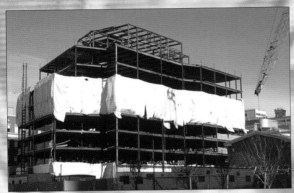

frédéric migayrou

A Plurality of Possible Worlds

Kolatan/MacDonald Studio, Resi-Rise
skyscraper, New York, 1999

Where does the reality of architecture lie? Does this reality still reflect the tools, language and uses of the discipline? Architecture that is built day in, day out, involving millions of square feet, is an architect-less architecture in which industry endlessly renews the self-same formulae in an ironic denial of the architect's craft. What is architecture's place when the claims of a neo-regionalist, traditional and vernacular architecture are the counterpoint to an extensive dispossession undertaken by the global economy, communications and the excessive planning of territorial management? How is a person to be an architect when the profession has seen its area of activity shrink to next to nothing?

Nowadays, architecture is obliged to deal with these problems of sovereignty, identity and legitimacy. It must win back its area of activity. It must redefine the conditions in which it stays close to the real, and become interventionist in every area involved in the industrial production of the building, from which it has been excluded bit by bit. All our dominant Western concepts of architecture (the way in which it has become a discipline, an area of learning and knowledge) have been adapted to an identity-related profession. Here, the principal architectural concepts are abstracted from the real building and at some remove from the complexity of the world.

Architecture has been modern ever since it gave way to the architectonic, to that desire to unify knowledge under one idea – ie the mastery of space and time defined by Kantian schematics. This gave an independent, ideal foundation to architecture, which, at the end of the day, has never been challenged. Architecture has always been postmodern in its failure to perpetuate this basic grammar, in highlighting its finest achievements in failure, drift, falsification, in the hijacking of the codes and standards by which it is determined.

The general extension and ubiquity of the urban space, the absence of any distinction between city and non-city, the increasing muddle between public domain and private space, and the standardisation of the economic fabric, information networks and cultural values – all these suggest that the world is a rational and continually expanding space. These days, continuous, unilateral urban-ness is an obvious fact, and the expected standardisation is now in effect. Normalisation goes beyond all predictions and forecasts, and the logical systems of trade

and services have increased ad infinitum the number of labels, marks and brands, in the end creating the unity of a worldwide culture where a growing number of values now forms the new unity of a symbolic world being shared by one and all. This unexpected form of universality has taken on the form of globalisation, the reign of an undivided economy that is no longer even the object of any political or ideological debate.

Confining the architect's work to that of a building process, a construction that invariably presupposes an availability of space, and turning architecture into an unambiguous art of space, is to be at the hub of a contradiction that has been evident throughout the history of Modernism. Paul Virilio put it in a masterful way: 'This geodesic faculty of defining a unity of time and place for activities now clashes openly with the structural capacities of means of mass communication'.[1] Nowadays, space is dimensionless; constantly redefined in tune with our technological capacities of configuration, it no longer involves measurement.

Globalisation is less an economic fact than a system of exchanges, which, in real time, reconfigure all decisions, be they political or economic. Architects who have long been dispossessed of any capacity to intervene, now work at objectivising the permanent scrambling of information that fuels the public domain. Cities, these days, are thresholds, or 'ports', to borrow from computer vocabulary. Globalisation is thus shifting all the old hierarchies and reforming an open field of decision-making, where each and every intervention is at once local and borne along by the limitations of the overall structure. By the look of the incredible diversity of the issues being

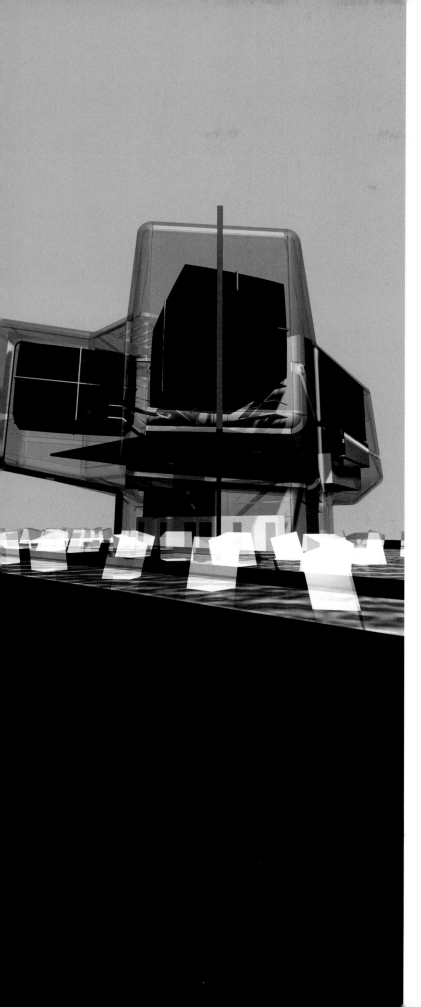

Grégoire & Petetin, Individual-Global
Home, Berlin, 1996/2000 (left)
Didier Faustino with MH Fabre and
S Metay, Ambassador of Portugal,
Berlin, 1998, project (right)

outlined by research architects, they are gathering together around the same established facts and the same postulates:

- the emergence of an immediate culture and a pragmatism of urban-ness, a new cognitivism;
- the co-existence of many forms of localism in an unprecedented space-time pluralism;
- a generalised recourse to models of morpho-genesis and calculation.

Globalisation invites us to think in terms of a plurality of possible worlds. It is imposing a hybrid, local and plural praxis on architecture. It is time to invent a non-standard form of city planning, a meta-constructivism of urban morphogeneses.

Translated by Simon Pleasance and Fronza Woods

Reference
Paul Virilio, Collection 'L'espace critique', Editions Galilée (Paris), 1984.

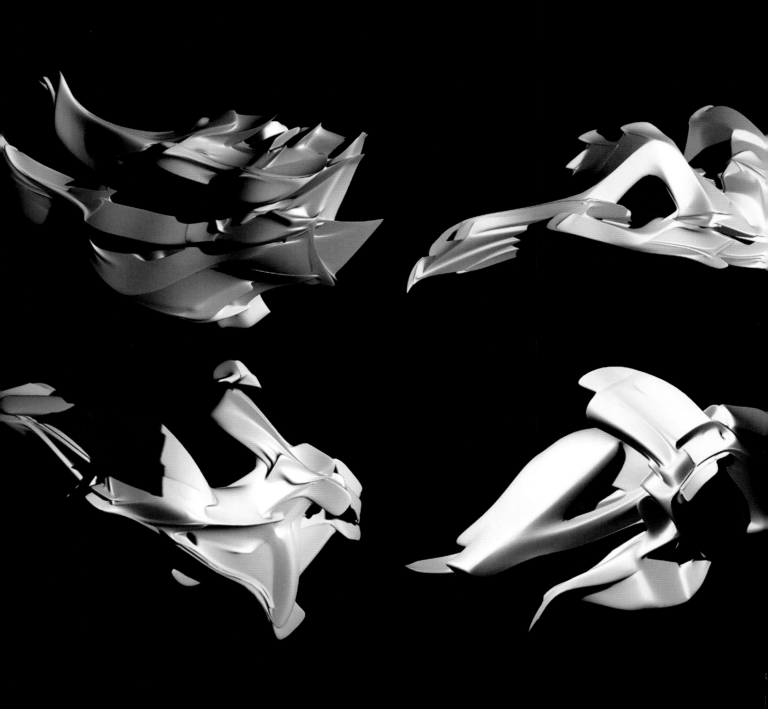

marcos novak

Invisible Architectures: An Installation for the Greek Pavilion, Venice Biennale, 2000

Composite Image, 1999

Elsewhere is a negative mirror. The traveller recognises the little that is his, discovering the much he has not had and will never have.

Italo Calvino, from INVISIBLE CITIES, Minerva (1997)

And all shall be well and
All manner of thing shall be well
When the tongues of the flame are in-folded
Into the crowned knot of fire
And the fire and the rose are one.

TS Eliot, from 'Little Gidding' (1942)

As we start our new millennium, we find that we live in a new, technologically augmented spatial continuum, a multidimensional spectrum spanning manifold ranges: from physical to virtual, from visible to invisible, from static to liquid, from handmade to generative, and from passive and innocent to interactivated and autonomously intelligent. The usual architectural and artistic responses no longer suffice; ordinary objects and forms appear reactionary and inadequate in dealing with the transarchitectural challenges facing a worldwide population carried away in the frenzied transition from a wired information society to a society of wireless global virtuality.

Even before invoking the question of technological, rather than merely Platonic, virtuality, it is evident that the information based upon which we construct 'reality' is severely limited. Our sensorium only detects a tiny fraction of the electromagnetic spectrum. Most of reality is invisible to our senses, and what we perceive is but a morsel of the whole. Technological virtuality gives us access to even larger worlds. Never before have we been able to see so far, and yet never before have we been so aware of our blindness.

Just how blind are we to the full extent of what exists? Even if we limit this question to that which can be sensed, the answer is humbling. Our senses respond to energy fluctuations in the electromagnetic spectrum. Of this spectrum we can detect only one part in 300,000,000,000,000,000,000,000,000,000,000,000, or $1/(3 \times 10^{35})$. To understand just how small a part of the whole this is, it is helpful to relate it to something with which we are already familiar, such as the width of a grain of sand. If we envision all that we can sense as a grain of sand, and calculate the full extent of the electromagnetic spectrum as a multiple of that small module, the extent of the entire spectrum would be far greater than the diameter of the visible universe, by an enormous margin. In fact, assuming that the diameter of the visible universe is 30 billion light years (twice the distance to the Big Bang), and that we live 36,500 days (100 years of 365 days), we would have to traverse the diameter of the universe 2.6 times each day of our lives in order to cover it. Our construction of reality is based on accessing a single grain of sand within that vast distance. Time, dimension and virtuality expand the range of what there is to be sensed and further underscore our limitations. Consciousness as neural 'process' and 'qualia' as the co-ordinate axes of an n-dimensional space of consciousness further enlarge that range. Invisible reality vastly exceeds visible reality.

The ongoing project of 'Transarchitecture', as I have posited it in previous writings and projects, is to set aside confining definitions of modes of science versus expression, pure research versus utilitarian application, or any such false dichotomies, and to pursue investigations into the unexplored territories of virtuality and the invisible wherever they may lead. As an item of both discourse and practice, 'Invisible Architecture' grows out of 'Transarchitecture' but does not supersede it, just as 'Transarchitecture' evolved from 'Liquid Architecture' but does not replace it. In this spirit, the installation I prepared as the centrepiece of the Greek Pavilion at the Venice Architecture Biennale, 2000, where I represented

Greece, is a next step in the attempted fusion of the virtual and the actual through the mediation of the invisible. For architecture, it proposes the notion of 'Invisible Architecture' per se; for art, the notion of 'Invisible Sculpture'; for technology, the notion of 'Invisible Interfaces'; and for science, the challenge of constructing instruments by which 'Invisible Realities' can be made accessible to an expanding human sensorium, for the sake of assisting us in the development of the intuitions that guide us to whatever realities we do access.

This installation explores a cluster of ideas related to virtuality, eversion, and the generalised invisible. More specifically, it explores how virtuality can be 'Everted' into physical space as invisible form rendered in what I call 'Sensels': sensor-elements or regions of sensed space understood as output, not just input. Invisible forms are created by the interactivation of space by sensor/effector pairings arranged to produce synaesthetic awareness of the virtual in ways that free it from its imprisonment behind screens, and cast it into our midst, in or out of doors, come rain or shine. 'Eversion' is the term I employ to describe a motion complementary to the familiar notion of immersion. Whereas 'Immersion' describes a vector moving from ordinary to virtual space, 'Eversion' describes the counter-vector of the virtual leaking out into the actual. Eversion predicts that the content of augmented reality and ubiquitous computing will be the population of the physical world with phenomena and entities first encountered in virtual space. There are numerous ways of achieving this: liquid, animate forms can be frozen and constructed; information can be projected upon hypersurfaces; data-driven mechanical space and surface structures can be used to create a new, digitally interactivated and kinetic tectonic form. Each of these options has its place and promise, and yet falls short of the full potential and unbearable evanescence of virtuality, the immateriality of pure presence. Clearly, the most daring, radical and elegant option is to render the virtual present and precise, but invisible. Invisible architectures, invisible sculptures, invisible interfaces: the reanimation of the world by worlds beyond worlds.

This installation consists of a series of interrelated elements: a) a core of algorithms generating b) a series of virtual, liquid forms that are displayed on c) a large video display, accompanied by d) 'Transactive', navigable, spatialised audio controlled by e) a series of five small and f) two large invisible sculptures, acting as g) invisible interfaces to virtuality and placed in direct juxtaposition with h) four suspended rapid-prototyped forms derived from the projections of i) a single four-dimensional form created by extruding one of the virtual forms into a fourth spatial dimension. Ironically, the element that was to be the armature and culmination of the physical realisation of the installation, a 3 x 7 x 3 metre screen wall derived from the same four-dimensional form and built using numerically controlled milling machines, was not realised due to the invisibility, at the last moment, of promised funding.

In ordinary space, the installation consists of three regions: a plane of interactivity, a plane of projection, and a space that is created between them. The plane of interactivity is created by a light-bar carrying five invisible sculptures. Suspended above the light-bar are four rapid prototyped physical forms. The five invisible and four visible forms are thus arranged in an alternating a-b-a-b-a-b-a-b-a rhythmic structure.

A large video projection displays algorithmically generated liquid forms, realisable only in the space of virtuality. The space behind the screen is the world we normally explore via what has come to be known as immersion. From these forms, one is selected for further development. This form is extruded into a fourth spatial dimension, and subjected to various 4-D transformations. In order to do this, both the geometry and the topology of the object are altered to include four-dimensional information. While this new 4-D object is inherently invisible to us in its raw form, it can be seen under projections. Given four spatial dimensions,

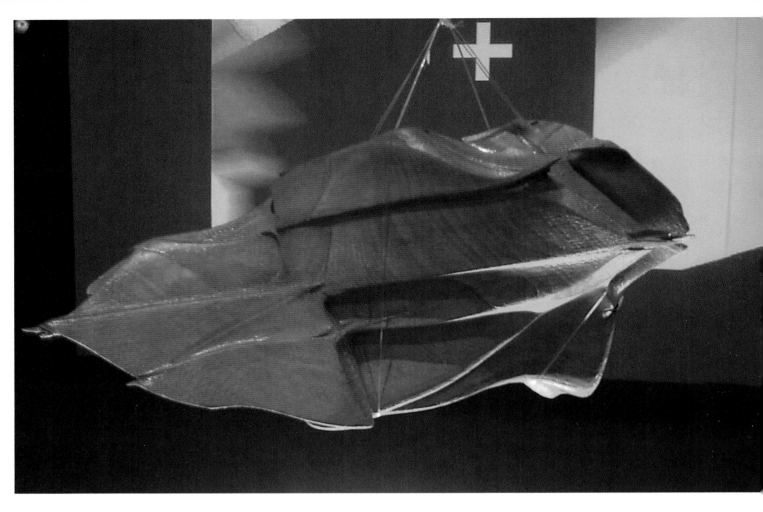

←x,y,z,w→, it is possible to construct three-dimensional projections by selecting three dimensions at a time. The suspended objects are generated using the ←x–y–z→, ←y–z–w→, ←z–w–x→, and ←w–x–y→ projections and are fabricated using a process called LOM (Laminated Object Manufacturing), whereby thousands of sheets of adhesive paper are cut by laser and pressed together into a solid, wood-like form. The solidity of these is contrasted with the evanescence of the invisible forms.

In the spaces between and around the four suspended 4-D objects, a series of infra-red sensors creates five invisible sculptures. Distinct forms in space are created that, although invisible, can be sensed synaesthetically, and which act as interfaces to the algorithmically generated sounds and projections. If one reaches into the field of the sensors carefully, following the contours of a particular sound, distinct shapes can be discovered. At the same time, these shapes act as interfaces, changing the contents of the projections, as will be described below.

The theme of the sensor-activated invisible is further elaborated at a larger size using another technology. Behind the interface bar, two red rectangles are painted on the floor to indicate the general location of two larger invisible forms that move from a sculptural to an architectural scale. Four infra-red cameras with integrated infra-red sources and visible-light filters shine light on the scene in a manner that is relatively independent of the light levels in the exhibition space. The computer tracks two cameras at a time, studying the common information they share, the intersection of what they each see, thereby defining invisible prisms, suspended in the space between the smaller invisible sculptures and the screen. As with the smaller invisible sculptures, their contours and interiors are linked to the algorithmic engine and act as interfaces to the specific generation of form, sound and image.

The algorithmic elements of the installation are arranged in a 're-entrant' cycle (to borrow a term used by Gerald Edelman to describe consciousness as process, in the context of neural Darwinism), one element affecting the other in a complex, indirect, non-linear manner.

The interactivity and 'Transactivity' of the piece are expressed in the control of the sounds and projections, both of which have a degree of autonomous behaviour, but which can be interrupted by viewers who come into contact with the various invisible forms. Before these can be explained, it is necessary to describe briefly the contents and behaviours of the projections and soundscape. First, in the case of the projections, the autonomous aspect consists of the rapid, alternating presentation of frames taken from a database of animations of liquid forms. Each animation suggests a different 'reality'. While in the present installation animations are used for reasons of expediency, the long-term intention is to employ living algorithmic processes. In any case, these 'realities' are presented at a rate as high as the computer is capable of rendering, in order to explore the notion of 'multiple time' in direct parallel to the investigation of higher dimensions in the rest of the work. The computer selects six or seven 'realities' from a much larger set of 'possible realities', and displays them on the screen faster than the rate at which the mind can form a conscious experience of a single frame. While any one image evades conscious recognition, its implication in an animated sequence, however disrupted, gives it a certain ambiguous persistence. Depending on the behaviour of the algorithm, the viewer can either perceive several realities simultaneously, or, at the other extreme, fuse them into an emergent 'reality' that is, however, absent from the database, thus suggesting that we can perhaps register more realities than we normally permit ourselves to consider, but that, even so, reality is still a construct of givens and of emergent relations.

The sound of the piece consists of algorithmically driven audio of several kinds: a general soundscape created through pure digital-signal processing without the use of any sampled sounds, evoking the fluctuations of electromagnetic fields; five kinds of sampled and processed voices, each associated with a particular invisible sculpture; instrumental sounds associated with the two larger invisible sculptures/architectures; and additional liquid-related sounds such as water-drops and rainsticks. All the sounds are heavily processed in ways that remove them from any sense of being overly literal, and are further altered dynamically through viewer interaction with the installation. Spatialisation is used both as a way of locating sounds in the exhibition space, so as to create yet another sense of the invisible, and as a filtering process by which to alter the character of the sounds into unfamiliar territories.

When the installation is undisturbed, its autonomous behaviour is calm and meditative. As users begin to interact with the invisible sculptures, however, this gradually changes. Caressing the contours of the invisible sculptures alters the sounds in gentle ways, but if the viewer presses too hard into the cores of the infra-red fields, the sounds become higher, louder, and increasingly altered. Simultaneously, the mix of the projections changes, initially just a little, but progressively more so. At the limit, the projections, which so far have only displayed liquid forms, begin to display alpha-numeric characters, fragments of a coded and broken language, just as the sampled voices become more shrill and pronounced: abstract repose has been agitated by literal interruption, but that interruption, engaging as it does the re-entrant loops of the algorithmic engine, signifies life.

Attending to all the sensor-tracking, audio-processing, video-tracking, video-projection, and overall algorithmic co-ordination of the various parts are four computers. In keeping with the concerns of the installation, these four machines are communicating with one another via a wireless network, literally filling the exhibition space with transmitted information and making it possible to control the installation remotely, from across the room, the Giardini, Venice itself, or the planet.

The horizontal arrangement of the elements of this installation juxtaposes the screen-bound virtual with the materiality of the rapid prototyped forms, and introduces the invisible as a condition in between these two poles. The vertical arrangement functions allegorically:

working from floor to ceiling one encounters a bed of sand, the suspended light-bar/interface bearing the invisible sculptures, the rapid-prototyped forms, the layer of algorithmic, spatialised sound, and, by inference, the inherently invisible four-dimensional form that is the implicit but absent centrepiece of the whole installation. Thus, in a manner analogous to Duchamp's LARGE GLASS (1915–23), the vertical allegorical structure is: earth (silicon), light (interface), dimension (materiality), space (aurality), and the inherently invisible.

While the technologies employed in the physical aspects of this installation allow us to envision a time in the not too distant future in which it will be feasible to build, at full scale, architectural form more complex than even that of Gaudí's Sagrada Familia, the proposition of the invisible as the newest of materials allows us to envisage how virtuality could inhabit the real Sagrada Familia, or indeed, cities and spaces at large, without offence. Still, such capabilities are simply enablers without content, and beg the question of how it is that we will imbue to our new instruments with meaning and relevance. This installation attempts to answer that question by peering into the darkness of higher dimensions and the realms beyond our direct perception and retrieving such things as might extend our awareness of larger worlds.

The explanations of authors tend to cloud direct perception and colour personal interpretation. This brief text does not presume to exhaust what meaning, if any, this installation may have, only to give the barest indication of what it comprises and what some of the questions that motivated its construction may be. This avoidance of inter-pretations does not indicate a lapse into solipsism:

quite the contrary: many of the motivations for this piece have to do with what is of increasing relevance to the world we are constructing as a shared and social effort. Rather, the avoidance of giving a preferred interpretation underscores the fact that another order of expression is present in this work, of a kind extremely significant to us, but of which nothing can be written. This expression is only articulated in the exact materials of any particular construction, and cannot be transliterated. The sum of these invisible architectures speaks in the specific combination of all their materials, virtual, physical and invisible, and that sum escapes language.

While in Venice for this installation, I came across a friend whom I hadn't seen for years, looking perhaps a little more gaunt and weathered than I would have expected. A day after I showed him the installation, and apparently motivated by what he'd seen, he sent me an e-mail message, letting me know that he'd recently lost his nineteen-year-old daughter to a car accident, adding, generously: 'philosophical reflections don't amount to much in the face of her loss. But right now I do feel that life is quite ephemeral, not like the solid 3-D surfaces heralded in the Renaissance, but more like a projection from some higher dimension'.

Of all the species of the invisible, the most remote is the 'Alien'; and of all the species of the alien, the most ineffable is the 'Alien Within'.

Acknowledgements

Special thanks to Elias Zenghelis, Commissioner for the Greek Pavilion at the Venice Biennale, and to David Harris and David Beaudry, without whose generous contributions the installation could not have been realised. Thanks also to Reg Gustafson, Chrys Halkides, Marco Hinic, Vincent Di Franco, Marco Brizzi and Maria Luisa Palumbo.

References

Gerald M Edelman and Giulio Tononi, A UNIVERSE OF CONSCIOUSNESS: HOW MATTER BECOMES IMAGINATION, The Penguin Press (London), 2000.
Howard C Hughes, SENSORY EXOTICA: A WORLD BEYOND HUMAN EXPERIENCE, MIT Press (Cambridge, Mass), 1999.

oosterhuisassociates

Bodyscan

Floriade Pavilion –
multimedia journey, 1999

First we need the body. Not your human body, but the 'product body'. We conceive and shape the body in weightless three-dimensional space, stretching, twisting and scaling it. We are developing a client-specific body style. In the design process, the product body transforms along its growth path.

The body is subject to a multiplicity of vectors. Multiple forces work upon it from the outside and from within. It is therefore a vectorial body; a uni-body with structural integrity. The body is described by variable sections connecting a series of reference points. This body knows only one detail for top, right, left and bottom. Its 'body-splines' are set by a formula and a series of subsequent parameters.

Then the body needs a skin, both exterior and interior. The construction is the adjustable spacer between the two. A seamless skin is wrapped around the body. Doors are cuttings out of the skin. Windows are warp-holes where the exterior skin folds back into the interior skin. The uni-body lands smoothly on the local skin of the earth after having exchanged data about their properties. Body-skin meets planet-skin.

The product-body is a spacecraft feeding upon data from its local and global site. During its life cycle we will feed it with fresh data from weather stations, the Internet and from direct input by users, who trigger sensors that play with light and sound. The body becomes an instrumental Play Station and is gradually transformed into a push-and-pull medium. Virtual worlds are the immediate extension of real worlds. The users experience the real and the virtual at the same time, like parallel worlds. Architecture becomes animated and unpredictable like the weather. The animate body displays real-time behaviour. Fresh data always calculate their values in relation to neighbouring data. Swarms of real-time data flock to the parameters inside the computer scripts. These formulas build the emotional factor of the body in real time. The building body finally goes wild.

'Trans-ports' Installation, Venice Biennale, 1999

The multimedia Floriade Pavilion, Holland's pavilion at the Venice Biennale, is an instrumental body that can be played by its users. When visitors enter the body, a variety of sensors feels their presence and triggers the electronic media. The building body gradually zips so as to exclude outside air and daylight. Electronic media take over and the visitor is immersed in a sequence of sectors. Strolling from sector to sector is a journey from real to virtual and back again. The full trajectory through the pavilion becomes a conversation between the visitor and the building body. The conversation is about the characteristics of northern Holland in relation to the Floriade flower exhibition. The journey is always specific to each visitor by virtue of the real-time programming. The building as an instrument offers active participation in the mediated experience, always calculating its effects and affects; there is never a dull moment. Leaving the building the body unzips, the electronic media turn pale, and daylight is back in command.

'Trans-ports' is a programmable vehicle that connects the virtual to the real. It is a data-driven, supple structure that changes shape and content in real time. This active structure is the first building of its kind to generate constructive strength when needed and to relax when mobile forces are modest. 'Trans-ports' is physically driven by computer-controlled pistons that operate in a co-ordinated fashion like a distributed swarm of filaments in a muscular bundle. While the changes in length of the flocking pistons are calculated in real time, the mediated interior skin adapts to a wide variety of content. The flexible electronic skin follows the movements of the data-driven structure. The skin is not a one-way display of information, but interacts with the users in a two-way exchange.

'Trans-ports' is a push-and-pull medium. It offers valuable broadcast time to its users on a timesharing basis. Individual and collective interaction creates a new bond between architecture and its shareholders. When

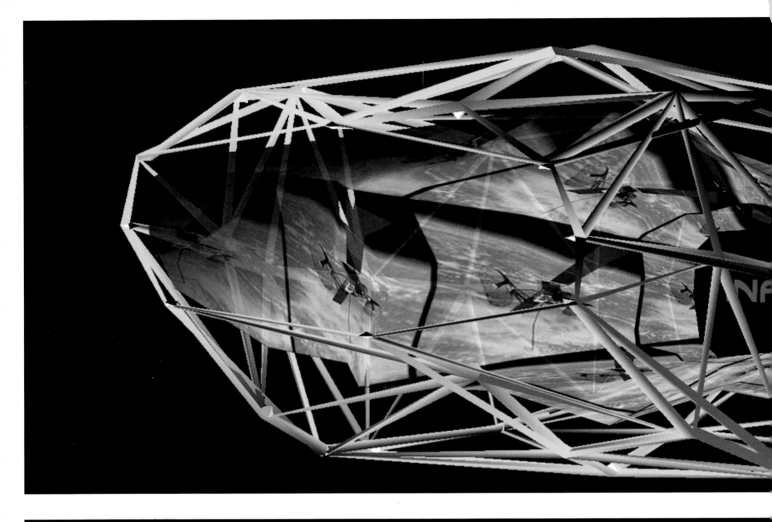

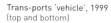

Trans-ports 'vehicle', 1999
(top and bottom)

technique digs itself deep into the building body, the form becomes animated in real time. Architecture goes wild.

'Hand-draw-space' is based on seven intuitive 3-D sketches that continuously change position and shape. The trajectories of the sketches restlessly emit dynamic particles. These appear and disappear in a smooth dialogue between the 3-D 'hand-draw-space' world and visitors to the installation.

The installation space can be visited and experienced through the web at:
www.trans-ports.com

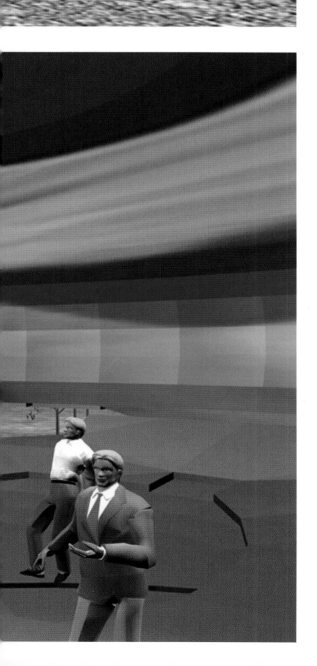

Floriade Pavilion:
external view (opposite top)
Iris opening (opposite bottom)
'Hand-draw-space' (below)

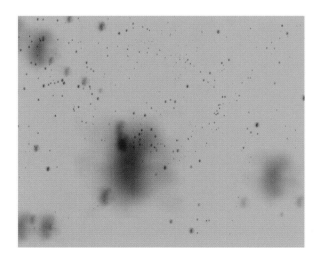

claude parent

A Paradox: Limits and Fluidity

Aeronef at Roissypole, 1994

When it first came into existence, thousands of years ago, architecture was concerned with stability. As a result, verticality, which allows static loads to be transmitted and which channels the forces that generate them, preventing a collapse of the structure, remains its one and only fundamental truth. Gravity dictated verticality, and when architecture began to be concerned with spanning, whether in the form of a simple beam or a bridge, the rule was to counteract lateral loads and to channel oblique forces by means of large masses perpendicular to the ground.

It was therefore inevitable that, for centuries, architecture expressed stability only through the means of verticality. One had to wait until the invention of the Gothic arch for the first manifestation of a diagonal transfer of static forces. But it was not until modern times, particularly through the use of reinforced concrete and steel, that the design of cantilevers gave us for the first time a conscious image of 'Disequilibrium'. From then on, starting in the 20th century, architecture made a definitive break with the past, a break that can be defined as a more and more intensive search for 'Instability'.

The notions of 'Instability' and 'Disequilibrium' naturally combine with that of speed to introduce the dimension of time in contemporary architectural research. It is therefore natural that architecture, after assimilating these new circumstances, these new demands, should now want to be dynamic. For the last few years, as if to confirm this new ethical stand, the Western world has adopted a fresh spirit by putting forward three new attitudes, three demands, three expectations:

• the search for extreme sensations;
• the notion of surfing;
• a sense of fun.

These three aspirations result from a desire for acceleration, a kind of hope to escape from the limitations of gravity through speed, while reducing as far as possible the use of mechanical devices. They express a new emphasis on, and repositioning of, the human body as a major centre of interest.

It is clear that the work carried out by Paul Virilio and myself in 1964, more than 30 years ago, anticipated all these demands in the field of architecture as well as those of modern choreographers in the realm of dance: rehabilitation of the body as a source of information, use of its mass as a motor; revelation of the potential energy of the inclined support; rejection of traditional systems of spatial reference through a tilting of the ground plane; multiple unfoldings of inclined planes; continuity, fluidity and succession; redefinition of the horizontal plane as the recovery threshold following a change of slope; replacement of the notion of space (external space–internal space) by the notion of surface (upper surface and sub-surface); the new pair of terms 'Surface and Sub-surface' instead of interior and exterior; combination of the two functions of circulation and habitation on one single supporting element according to the concept of 'Habitable Circulation'.

All these factors are now well established and are being researched extensively by architects and students through the use of computers, as is the case for instance with the Hypersurface, dECOi or NOX groups. But two specific analyses needed to be developed in more detail: the notion of 'Fracture' and the notion of the 'Limit'.

Fracture

In architecture, the notion of fracture challenges the supremacy of form as the one and only factor of the architectural proposition by carving it up along significant lines. The fracture allows one, after a number of real or suggested moves such as splitting, overlapping or sliding, to recompose the form differently and, in so doing, to allow a dynamic interpretation of the interlocking of component surfaces. It sets in virtual motion what is stable and immobile and prevents form from

Eglise de Neuve, 1964-66

displaying itself as an absolute certainty. It allows architecture to distance itself from formalism.

Limit

From time immemorial, architecture, pushed by the need to represent stability, has made use of the wall. As a direct result, inevitably, the wall took over the notion of LIMIT and, in an even more obvious and concrete way, that of CLOSURE. The latter, in turn, made considerable progress when, to symbolise power (privatisation of enclosed space) and the great monotheistic religions, it was declared sacred. The sacralisation of the vertical enclosure made it untouchable, universal, and legitimised the fact that architecture definitively erected itself as an obstacle. The notion of privatisation of the territory was further reinforced by that of inviolability. From then on, architecture became the best safeguard of private property and the land was subdivided into a multitude of enclosed spaces surrounded by impenetrable walls, around which it is hard to fight one's way.

A civilisation of the obstacle is imposing itself, opposed to the free movement of people. The city as we experience it is the outcome of this vertical occupation of available space; the urban drama is built around this deadly struggle between enclosed space (habitation) and interstitial linkage space (circulation). As a result, architecture has imposed itself as the major factor blocking communication. It is not surprising that in the age of Enlightenment, the French Revolution symbolically pulled down the walls of the Bastille even though this prison citadel was no longer in use.

One cannot help being impressed by the foresight of those philosophers who fought for the free circulation of ideas and often paid a high price

for the impertinence of their symbolic acts. In our days, despite appearances, the urban trap has closed in on us in a more totalitarian way; and even with the Internet, one still cannot see an end to the territorial crisis that stifles our desire for communication and freedom. Each building that is put up is a further obstacle to the movement of men, when it should really act as a bridge and link between them.

On the one hand, architects wish to work with layers, networks, accessible spaces freed from closed boundaries and on which the human species could fix itself freely and momentarily; on the other hand, developers continue to erect citadels in which we live behind walls. Our only safeguard against the universal ghetto is to think no longer in terms of volumes but in terms of surfaces; no longer in terms of rupture but in terms of continuity; no longer in terms of habitat but in terms of movement and trajectory.

The aim of architecture is to discover spatial manipulations that will guarantee the PRIVATISATION of places of residence and work without interrupting the continuity of movement. The key challenge for architecture is to invent structures that make it possible to protect the intimacy of human activities without ever resorting to enclosures. This need can be stated succinctly in the question: HOW TO LIMIT WITHOUT CLOSING? How to define limits without losing the fluidity of support structures and freedom of movement?

In order to answer this challenge, which seems at first to be so paradoxical as to be insoluble, one possible approach is to bring into confrontation many networks, layers, nets, in such a way that their superposition, their interpenetration constitute an impermeable system. As a result of the gradual shrinking in the mesh size of the networks, the place where they all come together eventually becomes impenetrable. All information signals, visual, olfactory, acoustic, tactile, can still go through such COMPRESSED ZONES: only the movements of man will be progressively stopped. The passage of people will be interrupted but information will flow.

Strangely, the tornadoes that hit Great Britain and France recently, and decimated the forests, created quite by chance a system of this kind. In certain places, the interlocking of felled tree trunks resulted in a tangle that neither vehicles nor men could penetrate. However, visual and acoustic communication remained possible. But it was still possible to consider climbing over the pile of trunks that had fallen to the ground. This dramatic caprice of nature therefore contributed to confirm, after the theory of 'habitable circulation', one of the fundamental hypotheses of the 'oblique function': that of the 'surmountable obstacle'. It offered a 'natural' manifestation of an architectonic system that responds to the desire to LIMIT WITHOUT CLOSING.

Translated by Colin Fournier

stephen perrella

Hypersurface Architecture: Age of the Electronic Baroque

Hypersurface Systems, Inc. Stephen Perrella, Laurent Paul-Robert, Vesna Petresin: studies for a virtual campus, 2000

Will the proliferation of technology serve to conjoin potential relationships within our environment, or will it create new realities altogether? Will the divisions that divide the realm of media from the realm of materiality continue to grow, or are there other possibilities on the horizon given the infusion and pervasiveness of technology? What deviations will there be for our cultural horizons in the growing instability between the real and the virtual? These sorts of question are taken up in the new architectural discourse, 'hypersurface architecture'. With a third volume in the works, two published issues by John Wiley and Sons in the Academy Editions series called ARCHITECTURAL DESIGN, HYPERSURFACE ARCHITECTURE, develop a line of inquiry into the uncanny new relationships between media and architecture.

In Robert Venturi's infamous National Football Association Hall of Fame for New Brunswick, New Jersey (1967), architecture and media were set into a relationship, as in most of his work, because each is fundamental to what configures our everyday environment. Venturi and Scott Brown have consistently considered the question of architecture's relationship to the world of everyday consumer culture. They are also well known for setting forth a distinction between architecture for architects (like the work of Frank Gehry) and architecture for the regular people who use it. Today, however, such distinctions are becoming ever more complex, to the extent that architecture might not be capable of recognising the new mutations and distortions that an onrush of consumer media will unleash upon its ever-softening forms.

Hypersurface theory considers new potentials that may reconfigure the relationship between media and materiality. These two realms have been divided much as an advertising billboard is systematically differentiated from the building it conjoins. Over the past decade, there have been significant shifts whereby the world of consumption (considered here as 'media') is overtaking its boundaries and at the same time, architectural form has also become delimited and smoothed. Because both of these realms are being altered simultaneously, it becomes a unique problem to comprehend possible integrations. Hypersurface is a way of understanding how to work within the play of a zone that opens up between media and matter. To do so entails an integration of theories that are non-Cartesian and non-dualist, and therefore borrows from the thought of Félix Guattari and

Gilles Deleuze, but also that of Martin Heidegger and the Deconstructionism of Jacques Derrida.

Hyper-
Precisely this sort of interpenetration of media and matter was anticipated in my work earlier this decade (The Institute for Electronic Clothing, 1990). The insights from that nascent project, which are still unfolding, prompt questions regarding the simultaneous play of form and image. Around 1990, a new and powerful technology had become available, allowing any form whatsoever to be texture-mapped with any image whatsoever. The result was that both image and form were destabilised, which was interpreted as leading to a crisis of representation. When one thinks of the powerful role that representation plays in the built environment, in terms of media and communication, it is no small issue to anticipate a fluxing proliferation of form and image, such that systems of representation begin to fail, or at least transmogrify. Think of, for instance, the role that paper plays when being written upon; how important it is that it be flat. If the world of media, which has clearly increased and is reaching saturation point, begins to infiltrate and overtake the architectural surface, then it will take a very complex surface condition to handle this scenario.

-Surface
The surface, in the considerations of hypersurface theory, anticipated that the infinite manipulability of form in the new technology would unleash the binds of traditional notions of form that are clearly Platonic and Cartesian. A decade later, the topological shift in architecture is seen clearly in

the work of Rem Koolhaas, Frank Gehry, Bernard Tschumi, Peter Eisenman, Greg Lynn and scores of leading architects whose work is emulated and largely influential throughout the architectural profession. Theoretically, this topological sensibility stems from Gilles Deleuze's book THE FOLD (1992).[1] It should be made clear, however, that the impetus behind much of this genre of work issues from the scope of manipulation made available to architecture by new software and hardware technology, in which the above group clearly revels. The last decade in architecture has seen many theoretical influences that loosen form from the grip of Platonic wholeness: Deconstruction, Deleuze (topology) and cyberspace, each challenged the deeply rooted assumptions about form that architecture has maintained.

Context

The main ingredient that motivates the flux of both media and surface is what drives our contemporary culture: capitalism. The incessant desire to instrumentalise all facets of life in a context of competition is what drives the media to insinuate itself into every fibre of human existence. The turning point where advertising becomes more real than any authentic local culture stems from pan capitalism and the unending drive in the marketplace to upgrade and satiate. Hypersurface theory recognises this impetus but also sees an opportunity in the way in which consumption and production might come together to create new forms of open-ended play.

Flux and Openings

One of the most significant aspects of hypersurface research is the claim that the realm of media develops independently of the realm of architecture; which is the same thing as saying that media and matter are split in our culture. If this case can be made, then the context of media being connected to consumer culture is a tremendous, growing force, especially when one thinks of the media as a complex between the televisual, the built environment and the Internet. Architecture on the other hand has developed independently from any actual involvement with media technology. Carving messages into stone seems hardly tenable today in the context of data profusion. Since then, architecture has stood its distance from the vulgarities of consumer

media, aspiring instead to a clarity of materiality (glass-and-steel Modernism). The accomplishments of Frank Gehry's Bilbao Museum in Spain, however, do more than express new possibilities in material fabrication. It might also be the case that his technological (and indeed artistic) achievement opens architecture to the flux of media. But in architecture, the world of Venturi is far from that of Frank Gehry. Hypersurface architecture anticipates an entire new realm opening between these two icons of architecture, but not motivated by architects alone.

Hypersurface

If architecture becomes the site of an integration between media and material surfaces (see the work of Lawrence Ko in Times Square, New York), then this hypersurface becomes a critical juncture, a sort of crossroads between space, time and information. It will become space-time information as one integrated fabric. The link between consumer culture, and all of the media that this entails, can be brought to bear on the surface fluctuations of the topology movement now underway in our profession, then many of our traditional dynamics will give way. We will need new methods to engage the reciprocal exchanges between these two realms and this is not currently part of our dualistic repertoire of understanding.

To consider best the sensibility or the 'logic of sense' of hypersurfaces we will require new modes of experience and social formation. Much of this is already being considered in the context of cyberspace, but of course that realm is one that is disembodied (again, part of our dualist nature). So it may be fundamentally incorrect to consider the cyberspace of the World Wide Web as a realm

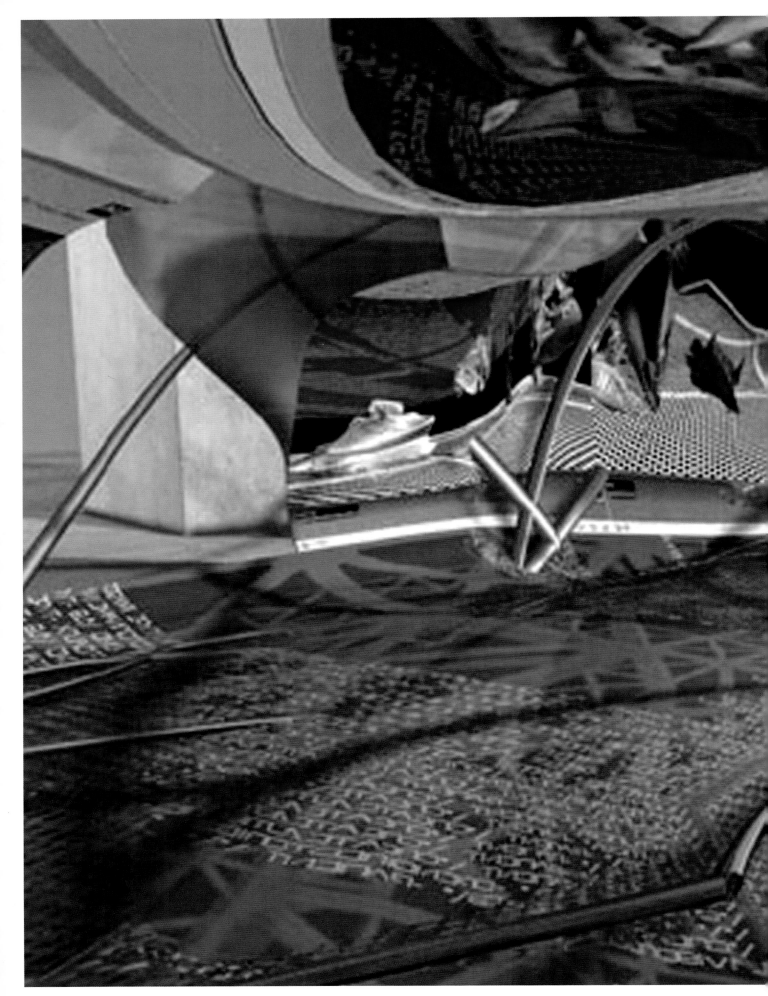

Hypersurface Systems, Inc. studies for a virtual campus, 2000

divided realm from that of the real world. As has been expounded here, both exist simultaneously. And this is our point of departure, a given condition, a superposition-as-ground that loosens any future consideration of architecture in relation to culture. Hypersurface accepts the superposed real/virtual split, but tries to open the void between and work from the middle out. Hypersurface theory evacuates the dualism between real/virtual in favour of a more open ended architecture that is inclusive and inviting of the media onrush, but also invites the onrush of topological surfaces that will necessarily problematise the mere communicative effect of media. When a radical media meets an ocean of waves in material form, then a new fluxing surface erupts. It is upon this surface that we will both need to read and write ourselves.

Reference

Gilles Deleuze, THE FOLD: LEIBNIZ AND THE BAROQUE, University of Minnesota Press, 1992.

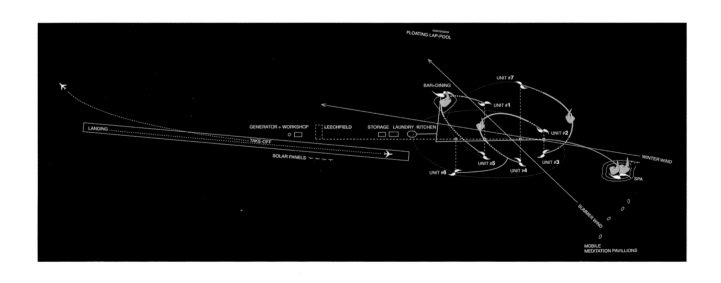

FLOATING LAP-POOL

UNIT #7

BAR+DINING

UNIT #1

GENERATOR + WORKSHOP   LEECHFIELD   STORAGE LAUNDRY KITCHEN

UNIT #2

LANDING

TAKE-OFF

WINTER WIND

SOLAR PANELS

UNIT #5

UNIT #3

SPA

UNIT #6

UNIT #4

SUMMER WIND

MOBILE
MEDITATION PAVILLIONS

┌─────────────────────────────────────┐
│ ГОЦ   │
├─────────────────────────────────────┤
│ Okavango Delta Spa, Botswana, 1998-2002 │
└─────────────────────────────────────┘

Site diagram (bottom)
Seven thatch-roofed guest pods are placed in natural clearings in the papyrus beds that line the delta. Service facilities are located adjacent to the aeroplane runway on the main island. Buoyant wood and fibreglass tracks weave through the papyrus, connecting pairs of units to the three termite-mound islands. A floating fibreglass spa is tethered to each pod. An infrastructural grid of waste pipes, septic tanks and pumps is submerged and runs along the delta floor connecting each pod. Wastewater is pumped to a leach field on the main island. The spa is made up of a series of fixed (bar, dining pavilion and guest pods), tethered (buoyant fibreglass spas and tracks), and free elements. Four mobile 'meditation pavilions' and a crocodile-resistant lap pool powered by a low-speed outboard motor can be manoeuvred through the channels or docked in the shade of the bar roof. The lap pool, a steel frame lined with steel mesh, allows guests to swim in filtered delta water. There is a bentwood deck for sunbathing.

This holistic health spa in the Okavango Delta in Botswana integrates two current trends in tourism: an increasing demand for eco-tourist destinations, and a spa boom triggered by pervasive media attention to stress-related ailments. This project combines an extreme African wildlife experience with the spa programme.

The site is deep in the Okavango Delta, a thin veneer of water covering some 15,000 square kilometres of an otherwise arid terrain, the Kalahari Desert of northern Botswana. Under the Kalahari sun, 95 per cent of the delta water evaporates annually. While the outer edges of the system fluctuate with seasonal rains, the inner zone, where the spa is located, is a perennial swamp. Floodwaters rushing southward from Angola replenish the region in winter. As the floodwaters recede, fresh grazing land is exposed. Vast migratory herds including elephant, zebra and wildebeest, traverse the terrain, following the constantly shifting pastures. Hundreds of abandoned termite mounds pepper the region. In fact, the islands that protrude above the delta waters were tectonically assembled over many centuries by millions of termites. No tracks for vehicles penetrate this deep into the delta swamps.

Bedrooms
Daytime temperatures during the peak
tourist season often exceed 90 degrees.
Thatched roofs are oriented to maximise
shade and take advantage of shifting winds.
A buoyant fibreglass spa moves with the
fluctuating water level. Water is filtered and
pumped into a solar collecting drum, placed
up high on an aluminium tripod at roof
level. Two pivoting arms feed heated water
to the oversized tub, shower and basin.
High-tech tent fabric and mosquito netting
can be drawn in a lightweight aluminium
track along the edge of the roof overhang,
following the thatch profile. The degree of
enclosure and shade is adjustable.
Extended overhangs allow areas of water to
be incorporated into the enclosed space

Situated on the rocky, west coast of Norway, the new fishing museum represents the long-standing marine and fishing culture of the area. Sponsored by a private foundation, it is connected directly to the people of the area by its function.

The site itself is relatively free of other structures and overlooks a saltwater inlet and a small collection of traditional coastal buildings. Rather than recreating an institution solely for the purpose of display, the new museum is a more neutral, sculptural form, placed into the landscape. The design is reminiscent of the simple structures developed locally by the fishing industry, yet articulated in a contemporary manner. The interior is flexible and open, allowing the contents to be rearranged easily over time. The museum is placed on the precipice of a small cliff, set perpendicular to the coastline, in contrast to the siting of many buildings along the fjord. The entrance is on the land-side of a long rectangle, whose far end comprises a giant viewing window overlooking the sea. Since the new museum is used primarily for exhibition purposes, it has few additional windows.

In recent years, many new industries have begun to replace the traditional forms of labour that sustained smaller, rural communities. Providing more than simply money and resources, these traditional industries were fused into everyday life, offering cultural qualities that cannot usually be fulfilled by new ones. As a result, there is a tremendous sense of nostalgia for old methods amongst the people of these areas. In Norwegian coastal communities, oil-based services and state-sponsored bureaucracies have replaced fishing and sea trades and many are looking for ways both to honour and explore their past. The most common method of exposing the past is by the superficial application of images upon the existing environment – postcards of the past. Another way is to create and enforce regulations to protect historical structures. The final method is to create museums housing artefacts from the past. In Norway, this is a common practice: the idea of setting aside a place for the future that is formed by remnants of the past can be found in nearly every city and town.

In the small coastal community of Karmoy, fishing was once an important way of life, and while it has not entirely disappeared, it is no longer nearly as crucial an industry. In order to create a place to focus attention upon this industry, a small group decided to build a museum to house its cultural artefacts and for use as a small educational institution for the community. The budget for the museum was based on a limited pool of resources.

Concrete is the primary building material (in contrast to the wood siding found on the surrounding buildings), which suggests that the fishing industry is not simply founded on a collection of quaint little houses, but is also a working, utilitarian society. The concrete has been treated with a fertiliser that allows moss to grow on its exterior surface over time, without damaging the concrete. The moist sea air is ideal for many forms of botanical growth, and the rocks and boulders forming the extensive coastline are covered in various types of fungi, moss and grasses, creating in the summer a beautiful pattern of greens, golds and greys. Over time, the building will become part of this pattern.

Large openings in the concrete structure allow for a kind of plug-in plan when future extensions become affordable. These are finished in glass where daylight is required, and when this is not the case, they are covered in a natural-finish plywood that weathers, like the concrete, over time. Across the largest opening, by the main entrance, the hole is covered by bracken-weave screens over glass. These are made using a local craft technique and the native, coastal shrub, eine, which helps to integrate the building with its surroundings. Bracken branches are normally used to acclimatise a building, woven so tightly that wind cannot easily penetrate, and the bracken is normally trimmed. Here, it is set in a contemporary way onto the outside of a concrete wall, and we have chosen to retain the leaves in order to give the facade a texture similar to the landscape around it.

Karmoy Fishing Museum, Karmoy,
Norway, 1999

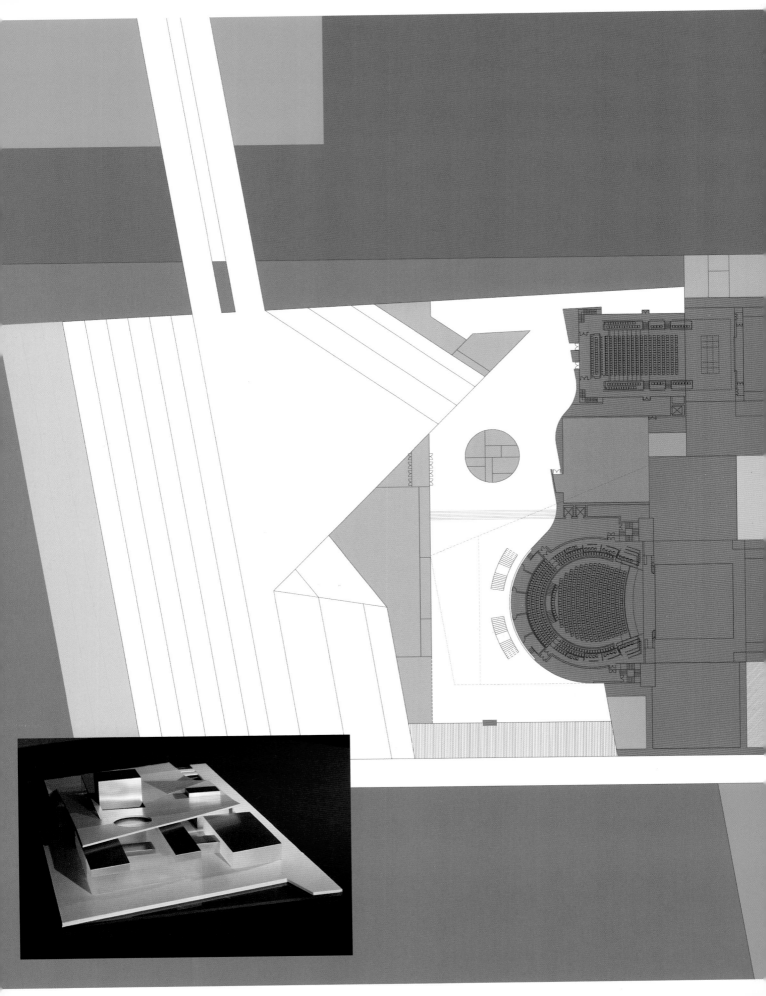

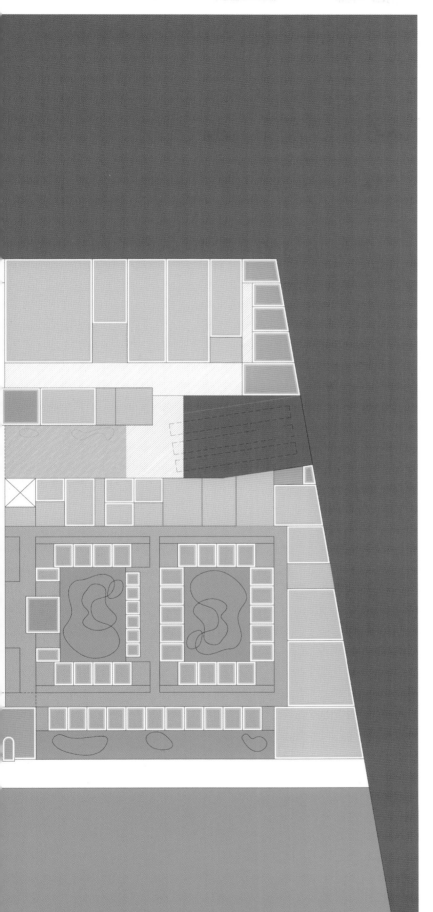

National Opera House, Oslo, Norway, 2000
Snohetta's winning design has been characterised as:

> a poetic and concrete response to a demanding assignment ... The design takes from the city and gives back to the city; it directs, but is nevertheless subservient, and puts people and the magic and power of the Opera House at the centre of the place. It creates an unexpected dynamic both externally and internally, to the benefit of lovers of opera and ballet, the city of Oslo and the international community.

A sloping roof surface rises directly from beneath the fjord. This vast platform can be traversed from the sea to the upper levels by the visitor. Fractures, stairs and the stage towers provide vertical movement, while the diagonal lines of the roof create an imposing yet humble composition, adapted to the scale of the city. Distinctive and unique, it forms an extension of the landscape surrounding the city, distinguishable neither as building nor ground.

softroom

Bio-diversity

Kielder Belvedere, Northumberland (1999);
Softroom's first new-build project.

Breaking into the world of building has never been particularly easy – unless you're lucky enough to get that fantastic competition win, or are blessed by a wealthy benefactor. Assembling a portfolio of built projects persuasive enough to guarantee a constant flow of work is simply not something that can be hurried.

Like many fledgling architectural practices, during the first five years of Softroom's existence, we have needed to be open-minded and flexible in our approach to finding work – which has led to a remarkable diversity in our output. In a relatively short period, we've worked on over 100 jobs, for many different clients. Some of those have been the sorts of building project a young practice might hope for in that time: private housing, a corporate fit-out, restaurants, retail, new-build work. Yet in tandem with producing built architecture, we have found ourselves involved in exhibition design, magazine illustration, creating advertising imagery, record covers and set design for television – even directing a top-ten pop video.

This scattergun method is only partly driven by economic necessity. It owes just as much to a desire not to be constrained by the traditional role of the architect. It is a question of capitalising on a slowly growing recognition that architectural skills are genuinely broadly based and can be successfully applied to a number of media.

A fluency with the concepts required to manipulate three-dimensional space on a computer is increasingly demanded of architects. By happy coincidence, the complex interwoven structures of the Internet and the powerful three-dimensional simulations required for science and entertainment both call for ordered, effective, spatial solutions. From our perspective, the 'virtual' realm is a territory to which architects are better placed than most to lay claim.

We were asked by BBC Television to create a virtual setting for their flagship sports programme GRANDSTAND. They wanted the presenter to be shown in a context with a generous sense of space. To us, it was a fairly straightforward exercise, and it seemed odd that such a giant corporation was not able to source such design material in-house. They had in fact spent many months calling on the skills of 2-D graphics artists, traditional set designers, computer modellers and even their own Virtual Reality department, without cracking the problem to their satisfaction. This seemed to vindicate our belief that there is indeed something extra that architects can bring to such a situation.

One of the great benefits of working on such public projects is the degree of recognition they can bring – a factor of immense importance to any young practice. This was demonstrated by the series of concept projects (a tree-house, supersonic private jet, tow-away desert island in a pod) that we designed for what was then a new start-up magazine – WALLPAPER*, which has, of course, subsequently been published and acknowledged internationally.

A valuable test-bed for ideas, the magazine gave us the chance to design freely, beyond the constraints of structure, planning and budget, while getting our name known to boot. Importantly, we were initially hired purely as illustrators – we were offering ourselves for hire as computer visualisers at the time – so what proved to be a fruitful collaboration had only arisen because, again, we were operating outside of the conventional architectural mould.

Such projects were also a valuable exercise in communication with a wider, general audience. A more extreme example of this was the brief we received to create a virtual world for a pop star. Although light-hearted, it was the sort of project that would only hold up to scrutiny if carried out with the sort of obsessive attention to detail that is the blessing (or curse) of any architect. It also provided excellent schooling in a whole new medium: video.

Having just completed our first new-build project, we have now reached the point where the reputation generated by our built work, together with our extracurricular activities, has led to invitations to pitch for bigger projects. But this is

Floating Island (1997); (top)
one of a series of concept projects
developed for WALLPAPER* magazine
Lolly World (1999); (bottom)
virtual environment for a pop star

not to say that we will now renounce any pursuits
that are not 'pure' built architecture.

Certainly, diversification could be considered a
distraction to the main task at hand. To look beyond
the accepted boundaries of a field of expertise
always carries the risk of turning one into the
dreaded 'jack of all trades'. To become proficient in
the area of building alone is demanding enough.
However, the process of seeking out alternative
applications for the palette of skills that
architecture requires can bring to light new and
unexpected opportunities, which not only provide
an extra outlet for our skills, but also extend and
enhance those talents in return.

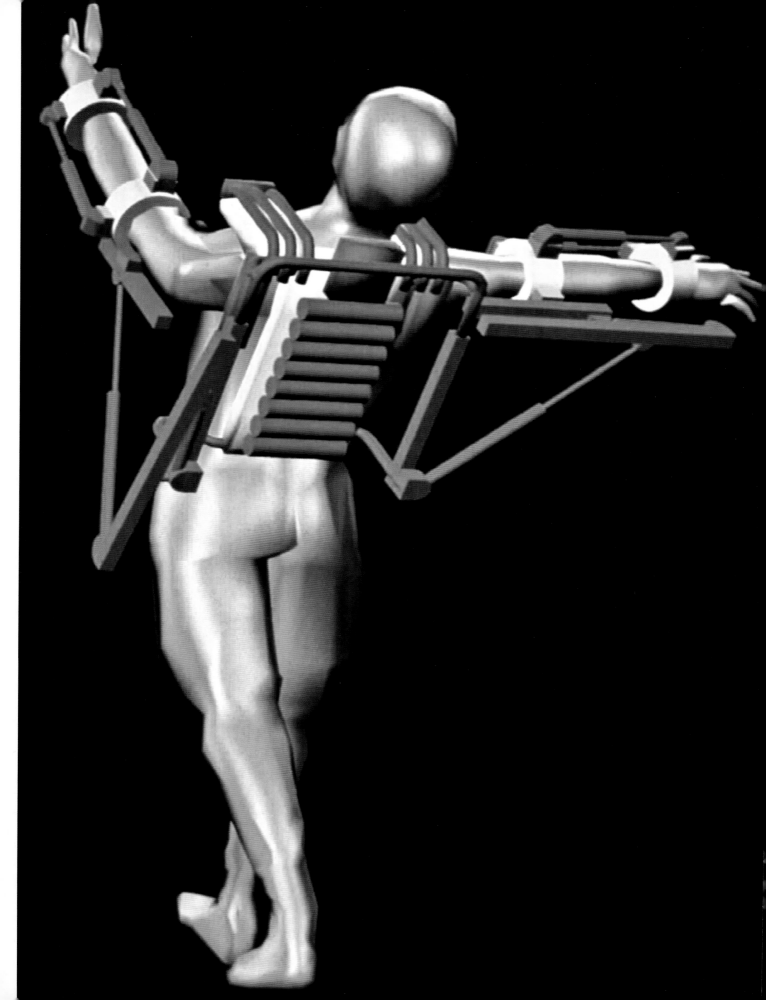

Zombies and Cyborgs: Absent,
Invaded and Involuntary Bodies
(extract from lecture delivered on 9 November, 1999)

Movatar (2000): rear view

Having made performances for the last 30 years, what interests me most is that conceptual expression is coupled with bodily experience. You have to take the physical consequences for ideas. So it's not just a matter of only representing the body symbolically or metaphorically, but rather that the body experiences the conceptual structure expressed. These alternative, intimate and involuntary experiences of the body in combination with technology are the focus of this discussion.

We've always had a fear of the involuntary, of a body that has no mind of its own; a body performing with the will of another. We've always been frightened of zombie bodies. We're also anxious about the notion of becoming increasingly automated or mechanised. In truth, however, we've always been zombies and cyborgs. We fear what we've always been and what we're increasingly becoming. We've never really had a mind of our own. The notion of free agency has to be understood in a structural, external way. To be an intelligent agent we need to be embodied and embedded in the world. We are part of an operational system whose intelligence is a manifestation of the complexity of the social structure and our cultural conditioning. Awareness and intelligence is that which happens between people, rather than within people. We need to re-evaluate our Platonic, Cartesian, Freudian notions of ego-driven bodies; we must come up with a concept of the body that goes beyond these outmoded metaphysical assumptions.

The notion of the cyborg has to be re-examined too, because when we evolved as hominids and developed bipedal locomotion, the two other limbs became manipulators and we constructed tools, instruments, machines and computers. In other words, the body has long been a prosthetic body, augmented by technologies. So, in this sense, we've always been zombies and cyborgs.

My performances initially explored different physical and psychological limitations of the body. For example, Event For Support Structure (1979) was a performance in which the body was compressed between two planks of wood. Its lips and eyelids were sewn shut with surgical needle and thread. I attempted to stay there for a week, but lasted for only three days. In another performance, the body was stitched up and tethered to the gallery wall with hooks into its back for seven days without drinking, eating, speaking, seeing. I could only hear, touch and smell.

The suspension events occurred in varying locations: in private gallery spaces, in remote locations, in different positions. In the Tensegrity Isohedron performance (early 1980s), none of the poles or the body was touching; everything was held together by the tension of the cables. The sound of the heartbeat and bloodflow were amplified, and the whole structure pulsated with these sounds. In Sitting/Swaying: Event for Rock Suspension (1980), the body's weight of about 70 kilos was counterbalanced by a ring of 18 rocks, each individually suspended from an insertion in the skin. It wasn't easy to find 18 equally weighted rocks and we had to use the lighter rocks where the skin stretched more and the heavier rocks where the skin was tighter. The body swung from side to side, setting up random oscillations in the rocks. It was perhaps the most meditative of the suspension events, and it was stopped when the telephone rang in the gallery.

In these earlier performances, the body was suspended, presented as a sculptural object. But now, the body becomes a host for a sculpture. For the Fifth Australian Sculpture Triennale in Melbourne, 1993, whose theme was site-specific works, an electronic object, the Stomach Sculpture, was constructed for inside the body. Rather than being a sculpture for a public space, it was constructed for a private, physiological space. This object was a capsule structure, 15mm in diameter and 50mm in length when closed, but when fully opened it was 75mm long and 50mm in diameter – closed, the size of a big thumb, opened inside the body, the size of a small fist. The sculpture extended and retracted, emitted a flashing light and a beeping sound: a choreography of sound, light and movement. It

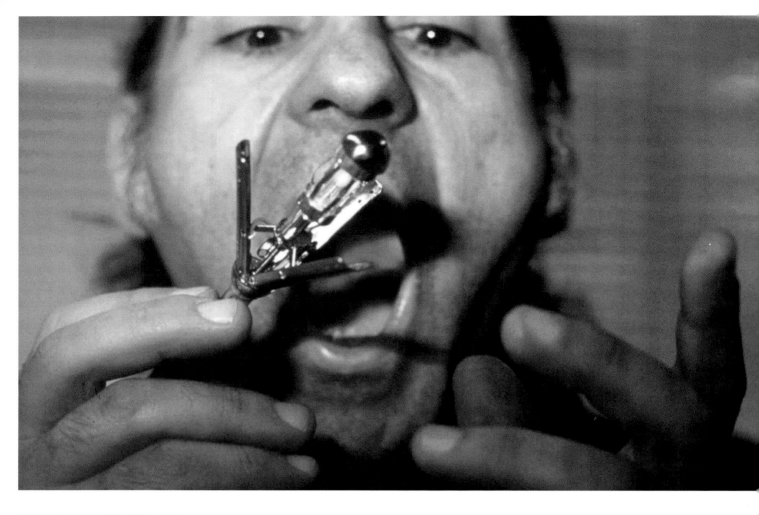

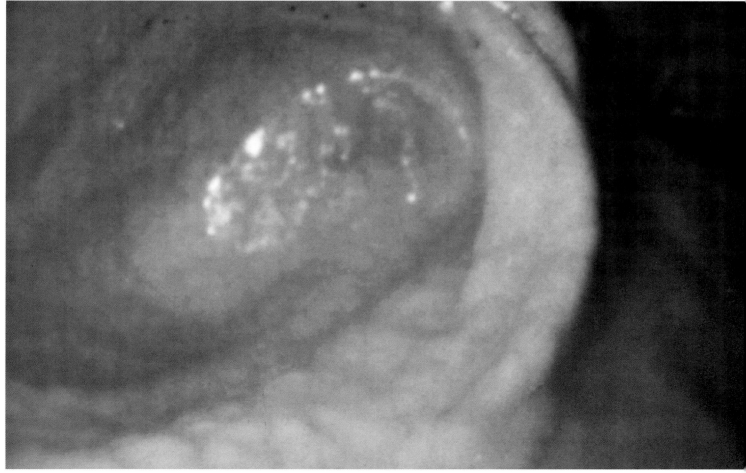

functioned within the wet, soft and previously dark environment of the body. Images were captured by an endoscope, also inserted. The mechanism was a worm-screw and link structure actuated by a flexidrive cable to a servo motor and logic circuit outside the body. This was made with the help of a jeweller and a microsurgical-instrument maker. Some of the internal links were made under magnification. The video was shot over a period of two days and six insertions were necessary. This performance incorporated a piece of technology into the body not through some medical necessity or for reasons of life support, but simply as an artistic choice. The body is no longer simply a host for a self but for a sculpture.

What we're seeing now is a body that has evolved as an absent body; a body whose senses are externally oriented; a body that has to navigate in the world. We tend to project mentally and our physicality is backgrounded unless we get sick, fall over, practise yoga. There are reasons for this feeling of being minds in the world beyond Cartesian notions of split minds and brains. These absent bodies have become obsolete in the sense that now the body cannot experience subjectively, either qualitatively or quantitatively, the information it is accumulating. It measures nano-seconds and light years. It can't subjectively experience this information. The body has constructed machines that out-perform it in precision, speed and power. Technology also accelerates the body, attaining planetary-escape velocity, finding itself in alien environments within which it is not designed to survive; so the body is obsolete in these ways. This absent, obsolete and invaded body now performs involuntarily in the electronic and extended space of the Internet.

Exoskeleton, constructed in 1998 as part of a residency in Hamburg, is a six-legged, pneumatically powered walking machine. The legs have 18 degrees of freedom. The locomotor, with both ripple- and tripod-gait modes, can walk forwards, backwards, sideways (left and right) and turn on the spot. It can also squat and lift by splaying or contracting its legs. The body is positioned on a turntable, enabling it to rotate about its axis. It has an exoskeleton on its upper body and arms with magnetic sensors embedded so that the arm gestures can select the different leg motions. There is a translation of limb to leg motions, and a transduction of human bipedal gait into a six-legged insect machine motion. The exoskeleton also extends the right arm with an 11-degree-of-freedom manipulator, capable of thumb and wrist rotation and individual finger movements, each finger splitting open to become a gripper in itself. The compressed air sound, the relay-switch clicks and the mechanical sounds are acoustically amplified. Choreographing the movements of the machine and manipulator composes the cacophony of pneumatic, mechanical and sensor-modulated sounds.

Until now, the body has been augmented by prosthetic bits and pieces attached (and once implanted). But what if the body becomes a prosthesis in itself? Imagine if we could construct an intelligent avatar able to access a physical body and manifest its behaviour in the real world. This would be both a possessed and performing body. And if this avatar is a VRML entity on a website, any body could log in at any time, from anywhere. The avatar could choreograph single bodies sequentially or clusters of bodies simultaneously, which were spatially separated but electronically connected to it. This intelligent avatar would be able to choreograph physical bodies, blurring the distinction between a virtual entity and an actual body. And if in addition to sensors on your limbs, you also had them attached to your facial muscles, then the avatar would not only be able to move, possessing the physical body, but would also be able to express its emotions through the physical body's facial muscle contractions.

Movatar was first performed for CYBER-CULTURES in the Casula Powerhouse on the 19 August 2000, using not a muscle stimulation system, but a pneumatically powered motion prosthesis, allowing 3 degrees of freedom for each arm. This

Exoskeleton (1998)

provided 64 different combinations of movement. The system enabled a 'GIF-like' animation of the upper body, whilst the legs were free to move under their own agency, pressing foot sensors to modulate the tempo or rhythm of the performance and varying the mutation rate of the avatar's evolutionary algorithmic engine. This set up a dialogue of virtual and physical gestures – of actuated, improvised and prompted motion.

Stelarc is Honorary Professor of Art and Robotics at Carnegie Mellon University and a Senior Research Scholar at The Nottingham Trent University. His art is represented by the Sherman Galleries in Sydney.

cLorindo testa

A Paean to Testa by Peter Cook

Bank of London and South America (1966)

The idea of artist-architect has appealed to many 20th-century commentators as an alternative to the creeping technocratic determinism that forms the basis of much recent architecture. Clorindo Testa's paintings and drawings have a powerfully spatial as well as dramatic quality – marvellously uncluttered and direct in comparison to the usual architect's 'art piece'. But then the same can be confidently said about his buildings. They demonstrate broad strokes of form and a heroic presence, but with a subtlety of touch that can be clearly seen in the way he articulates a series of openings, ribs or barrels, and the manner in which humorous extrusions from the main form seem to find themselves in just the right place.

Testa says of his student days in the 1940s:

... we had experienced, pleasant, learned teachers, whose teaching had absolutely nothing to do with current trends in architecture. I must have been in [my] fourth year at the university when I heard Le Corbusier speak. He became my model both in my university years and after graduation, for I never paid much attention to other architects.

Certainly there is a Corbusian attitude in Testa's strong carcass and the potential for other strong objects to wrap and fold into it. The cue to his fluency with such actions is to be found, once again, in the drawings. The action of climbing, waving, grasping or folding seems to occur in many of them. If one looks at the National Library (Buenos Aires, 1962), one can see (on an enormous scale) the same instinct for objects to come out from the shadows, call for your attention and then fold themselves back. Sometimes, this instinct to fold and tuck is carried to its extreme, and a piece of the building is completely buried in the ground before folding itself out from underneath.

In these ways, Testa is reminiscent of the early Arata Isozaki, during the period of his school and banks for Oita and Fukuoka in the 1960s. Both architects extended out from the inheritance of Le Corbusier far more flamboyantly than most (in Isozaki's case, via the intermediary figure of Kenzo Tange).

Another link, though perhaps coincidental rather than referential, exists between Testa's formalism and dynamic ability with extruded solids and that of the English Bowellists, notably Michael Webb. Tubes and vents are the more obvious elements with which to create such a forceful vocabulary, but to allow the major spaces themselves to wrap and fold and become part of the same exercise requires both boldness and control if it is not to become tiresomely eccentric. The Bowellists thought in terms of 'flow and form', creating an analogue between the internal rise and fall in pressure and sequence of action, a squeezed or filled balloon, defined by thick, concrete skin. Testa seems to do the same. In the library building and in the prize-winning scheme for a city, Auditorium for Buenos Aires, he does just this, and begins to draw our attention, by inference, towards the defined or 'contained' pieces of air between these objects. If looked at as 'white rooms', as opposed to the built 'black rooms', they have a highly evocative presence.

In critical terms, this all leads up to the masterpiece of Testa's output: the Bank of London and South America (Buenos Aires, 1960-66). The competition project was made in 1959 by Testa together with the office of SEPRA (Sanchez Elia, Peralta Ramos and Agostini) and the building was finished in 1966. The characteristics already alluded to are all here, but are given a programme and a degree of development (and presumably budget) that permit them to flower.

In a sense, though, the greatest achievement of the building is generated from outside the site. The building is at the intersection of two narrow streets in the business district of Buenos Aires. The corner condition of the building opens up towards the intersection, but dropping a great visor of concrete over one part of the opening. The other three corners therefore become apparent

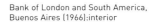
Bank of London and South America,
Buenos Aires (1966):interior

constituents of the 'room' made from this piece of city. This building makes exotic and brilliant use of a layer of fins, punctured by concrete panels and deep-set glass walls. It carries out the proposition of the bold cage of concrete with a degree of inventiveness so far unmatched.

The general proposition of the building is strong too, for it can be read as a system of two bands of trays separated by a void, or as a skilful combination of 'tree' growths. Within this series of propositions, the deftness of position and stylisation of such things as lifts, stairs, columns and fins is quite beautiful.

I first saw the scheme in illustration in the mid-1960s and was of course fascinated by it, but then the memory receded. After all, Argentina was a long way away, and I was unlikely to see it. The most pungent after-image was that of the shadows running into the rounded-off screen apertures and the strident fins.

By the time I confronted the reality in the 1980s, I had fallen out of love with the rounded corner and bold fin, feeling that Isozaki's big bank in Fukuoka had communuicated just about all that one could in this particular aesthetic. On seeing it, however, I found myself totally unprepared for the sheer spatial quality, the dramatic handling of filtered light and the 'corner' gambit.

This experience allowed me to draw two conclusions. Firstly: one should not presume that first experiences should be edited out by the breathless search for the 'new' aesthetic. Secondly: one should not trust books and magazines, for when the building is THIS good, they are a poor means of representing or explaining space and quality of theatre in architecture.

All photographs © Peter Cook

The house was built for a man who was born and raised on Motiti Island – an island visible from the coast of another, much larger land, the North Island of New Zealand. The spatial proximity of the two has not led to cultural homogeneity, however. The 30-kilometre stretch of sea between them has geographically isolated, and therefore historically insulated, Motiti from many of the devices of Western existence, including architecture.

Paradise Lost

One of the many stories of architecture starts at a time of innocence; a primal scene of uncorrupted naivety; a Garden of Eden, in which the first shelter was built – a simple hut. With the rise of luxury and the spread of vice, the purity of this unadorned building was corrupted. The hut no longer simply served its function; it became decorated with ornament. The naked body of the hut became clothed. Building became architecture.

To the world, New Zealand is paradise, an idyllic dream-world uncorrupted by the excesses of contemporary man – or by architecture. New Zealand is the tabula rasa, the clean slate. Its tradition is one of building rather than architecture. Indeed, New Zealand architecture is a contradiction in terms. What defines the local condition is not a certain architecture but a certain resistance to it.

Country and Western City

The island-country of Motiti is the same physical size as the island-city of Venice. Venice has more than 7,000 inhabitants, Motiti, just 30. Architecture has always belonged to the sophisticated domain of the urbane; its schools, galleries and publications – its spaces of discourse – are sited in the metropolis. The Rural Institute of Architects is nowhere to be found. Architecture is at a loss on Motiti.

Buildings that Talk

Motiti Island is Maori land. European constructs such as land titles do not exist. Land is neither bought nor sold and architecture has neither created nor destroyed the island. The relationship between the Maoris and the buildings that form their Marae (a rural space) is particular. One might be tempted to proclaim it as madness: in the manner of Doctor Doolittle, who spoke to the animals, Maoris initiate MARAE proceedings by speaking directly to the buildings.

Technology

The man had returned to the island, after a life spent working on the mainland, because he felt unable to comprehend a world so technologically modern that it saturates communication with information. On Motiti there are no cars, electricity, sewerage infrastructure, shops, currency, computers. The house, simply by being on Motiti, offers refuge.

Arrival

The airstrip and the jetty are on opposite sides of the island, and the house is orientated so that a door at each end greets both those who have travelled by sea, and those who arrive by air; two doors, but no front door.

Luxury Device

The modernist attempt to turn architecture back into building by removing the corruption of ornament and returning to function meant that New Zealand architects were able to participate in the international debate whilst preserving their regional tradition. In accordance with the buildings of its vernacular, New Zealand has always had a certain disregard for the luxury device that is architecture. A do-it-yourself culture of weekend extensions and impromptu beach houses accelerated with the arrival of Handyman stores. The self-build house on Motiti is sited in the context of a building tradition that undermines the distinction between building and architecture.

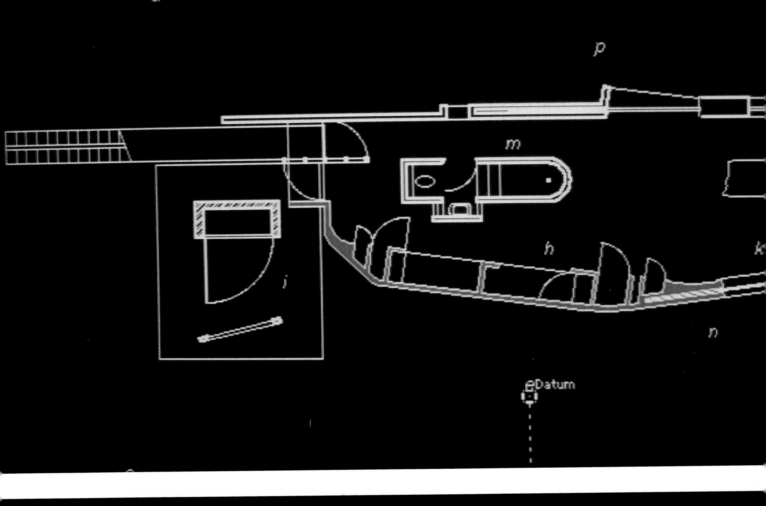

a

p

m

h

k

i

n

⊕Datum

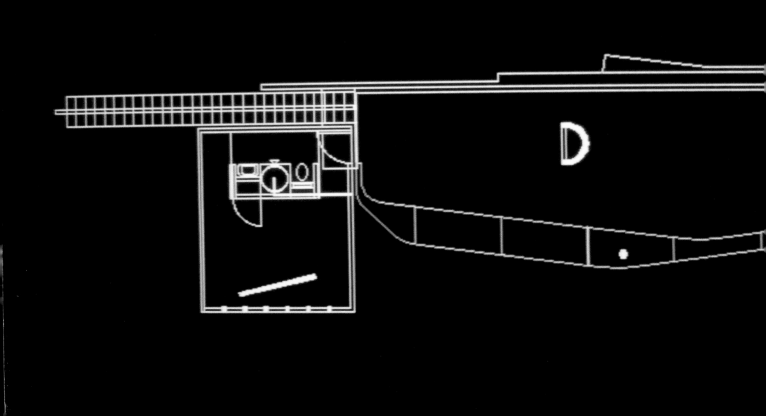

D

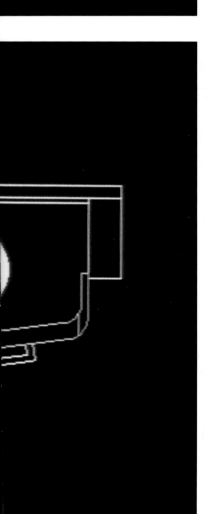

Motiti House: ground floor (top);
first floor (bottom)

House

The house has two principal spaces that do not touch: a reformulated whare (a traditional yet modern communal house) for the man; a motel room for his guests. Within the whare is a narrow concrete bathroom with overhead rainwater storage and a suspended kitchen. All building materials not dug from the beach were shipped on site via a cattle barge; the cows creating havoc during construction by eating the materials. The whare is defined on its southern side by a plywood wall, bent into varying sections for domestic appliances. This wall incorporates the spaces of living room, bedroom, laundry and storage.

The motel box is suspended above the whare, separated from it by a 100 mm seismic gap to accommodate the different harmonic frequencies. Here, one is reminded of that other distinguishing characteristic of building in New Zealand: the ground. The beauty of the natural landscape is the result of geological turmoil. Motiti lies near the faultline that runs the length of the country, creating mountain ranges, lakes, fjords, geysers and craters. From the roof of the house, seven other islands can be seen, including the nearby volcano, White Island.

phiLLip steadman

How the Electric Railways Shaped Los Angeles
(extract from lecture delivered on 14 October, 1999)

Robert Zemeckis' WHO FRAMED ROGER RABBIT? (1988) is set in Los Angeles in 1947. The wicked Judge Doom is plotting to buy Toontown and demolish it. His plan is to build in its place a monstrous eight-lane superhighway and to develop the land alongside. But the Toons resist. As detective Eddie Valiant (Bob Hoskins) says: 'Who would want to drive the freeway when they could take the Red Car for a nickel?' If you haven't seen the film, you'll be glad to know that it ends happily: Roger Rabbit arrives to help save the day, Judge Doom's evil plans are thwarted, and the Toons all escape back to Toontown through a railway tunnel.

The film refers obliquely to real places and events in the history of LA. Judge Doom, of course, represents the interests of the automobile and property lobbies. His superhighway is the Hollywood Freeway, the first to be built after the war. Eddie Valiant's Big Red Cars are the trains of the Pacific Electric Railway, which grew in the first two decades of the 20th century, and at its peak was the biggest urban rail network in the world. The system boasted more than 1,100 miles of track. Very few traces of it remain today, although if you search carefully you can still find fragments of the rails embedded in the tarmac of the city's boulevards. The most substantial relic is a short section of tunnel, completed in 1925, running from the Downtown Terminal on Hill Street in the direction of Glendale. Closed to the public, the concourses, booking offices and platforms are crumbling and covered in dust, and the tunnel and terminal are now used only as sets for the occasional X-FILES episode. This is the tunnel through which the Toons escape, on a Big Red Car – for it leads to Hollywood, to Toontown.

In the 1970s, a Washington analyst called Bradford Snell presented a report to the US Senate, in which he argued that public transport in America had been deliberately destroyed by the automobile industry, and specifically by the car manufacturers General Motors. 'Nowhere', Snell said, 'was the ruin from GM's motorisation programme more apparent than in Southern California.' GM and other car interests, according to Snell, had bought up the Pacific Electric and dismantled it, in order to sell automobiles. This account not only forms the basis for WHO FRAMED ROGER RABBIT?, it has since gained wider currency and continues to be repeated in documentary films and books – even in academic texts. It perhaps appeals to conspiracy theorists among supporters of public transport. But it is a total myth.

It IS true that a company in which GM had a shareholding, together with various oil interests, bought up the Los Angeles Railway (a separate system that operated Downtown) in 1944, and dismantled the streetcars. But they replaced them with diesel buses, which were manufactured by GM. GM's interest was in road transport, certainly, but it was in PUBLIC transport on the roads. Buses were being introduced even before the Second World War by the Pacific Electric because they were more flexible, and could perhaps slow the decline of the public transit system as a whole. By the 1940s, the old Pacific Electric was no longer an effective and popular system; indeed, it had been losing money and passengers since the late 1920s because of competition from the automobile. Angelenos took to their cars in preference, and were enthusiastic about the freeways. You might even say that the freeways went to their heads. If Zemeckis had wanted Eddie Valiant to be historically accurate, what he should have had him ask was, 'Who would pay a nickel to ride the Red Cars, when they could drive the freeways for free?'

References
Martha J Bianca, 'KENNEDY, 60 MINUTES, AND ROGER RABBIT: UNDERSTANDING CONSPIRACY-THEORY EXPLANATIONS OF THE DECLINE OF URBAN MASS TRANSIT', paper presented at 78th Annual Meeting of the Transportation Research Board, Washington DC, January 1999.

S Bottles, LOS ANGELES AND THE AUTOMOBILE: THE MAKING OF THE MODERN CITY, University of California Press (Berkeley), 1987.

Mark S Foster, 'The Model-T, the hard sell, and Los Angeles's urban growth: the decentralization of Los Angeles during the 1920s', PACIFIC HISTORICAL REVIEW 44, 1975, pp 459–84.